# Cleaning
# HACKS

## Your All-Natural, Go-To Solution for Spots, Stains, Scum, and More!

Sarah Flowers

Adams Media

New York   London   Toronto   Sydney   New Delhi

For my mom, who would be so proud.

Adams Media
An Imprint of Simon & Schuster, Inc.
57 Littlefield Street
Avon, Massachusetts 02322

First Adams Media trade paperback edition June 2019

ADAMS MEDIA and colophon are trademarks of Simon & Schuster.

For information about special discounts for bulk purchases, please contact Simon & Schuster Special Sales at 1-866-506-1949 or business@simonandschuster.com.

The Simon & Schuster Speakers Bureau can bring authors to your live event. For more information or to book an event contact the Simon & Schuster Speakers Bureau at 1-866-248-3049 or visit our website at www.simonspeakers.com.

Interior design by Colleen Cunningham

Manufactured in the United States of America

10 9 8 7 6 5 4 3 2 1

Library of Congress Cataloging-in-Publication Data has been applied for.

ISBN 978-1-5072-1043-7
ISBN 978-1-5072-1044-4 (ebook)

# CONTENTS

# INTRODUCTION

Feeling overwhelmed by how long it takes you to clean your home? Worried about the potentially harmful chemicals in so many store-bought cleaners? It's time to embrace *Cleaning Hacks* and make cleaning faster, more natural, and easier!

- Did you know you could clean 99.9% of the bacteria off your sponge by putting it in the microwave for just 2 minutes?
- Or that you could use a rubber glove to clean up pet hair instead of a lint brush?
- Or that waxed paper can be used to make your faucets and sink fixtures shine instead of a chemical polish?

Cleaning can seem like a never-ending task—make it easier and faster with these more than five hundred simple and all-natural cleaning hacks. All-natural cleaning may seem like a new trend, but these DIY recipes and tricks have been around for generations and are still going strong because they work. The cleaners and methods in this book are safe to use around children and pets, and your home will be just as clean, or even cleaner, than before! While standard commercial cleaners can actually cause or aggravate existing health conditions, natural cleaners can even help alleviate symptoms such as allergies, asthma and other respiratory problems, autoimmune diseases, and more.

*Cleaning Hacks* is packed with short hacks, which are simple tips and tricks that quickly solve a common problem; lists that go more in-depth by offering various solutions for one cleaning project; and DIY recipes to make your own cleaners with affordable ingredients you know you can trust to clean and disinfect your home without sacrificing your family's health and safety.

Combined, all the different hacks in this book will help you save money, reduce your exposure to dangerous ingredients found in commercial household cleaners, and streamline your cleaning schedule to give you more free time to enjoy other activities. Let's get cleaning!

# 1. NATURAL CLEANING 101

If you're new to natural cleaning, you may feel intimidated by the transition from readily available commercial cleaners to a whole new method of cleaning. In reality, it isn't any more difficult than using harsh chemicals, and it can even prove to be simpler, faster, and more cost-effective. If you're worried about cost, you can transition to natural cleaning in incremental steps. Continue to use your standard cleaners until you run out so you don't waste money you've already spent. Then you can slowly replace those old cleaners with the supplies discussed in this book. And remember, these all-natural options can improve your family's health and quality of life.

# Basic Cleaning Supplies

While it's true that store-bought natural cleansers can cost more than their conventional counterparts, many natural cleaners use common and inexpensive ingredients that you may already have in your home—so consider making your own! Any ingredients you may need to purchase are readily available and usually cost less and last longer than chemical cleaners. Here are some basic supplies you should have on hand to transition to natural cleaning:

- ❍ All-natural dish soap (store-bought or homemade)
- ❍ Baking soda
- ❍ Borax
- ❍ Castile soap or Sal Suds
- ❍ Containers for DIY cleaning recipes, preferably glass
- ❍ Cooking salt
- ❍ Distilled water (optional)
- ❍ Essential oils (optional)
- ❍ Food-grade diatomaceous earth
- ❍ Hydrogen peroxide (3%)
- ❍ Microfiber cloths
- ❍ Polishing cloths
- ❍ Vegetable oil
- ❍ Vodka or rubbing alcohol
- ❍ Washing soda
- ❍ White vinegar

You probably already own a good number of these ingredients, and if not, you could buy them at a local grocery store. Let's take a closer look at some.

## Baking Soda versus Washing Soda

**Baking soda** (sodium bicarbonate) is perhaps the most common and useful ingredient in natural cleaning. It's abrasive, making it a fantastic natural scouring agent. It also helps absorb moisture and neutralize odors and can last up to 6 months when stored in an airtight container. Never store baking soda and vinegar mixtures in a closed container. When these two ingredients are mixed together, they form an explosive reaction, which can prove dangerous in enclosed spaces.

**Washing soda**, also called *sodium carbonate* or *soda ash*, is a natural cleaner, water softener for hard water, and degreaser with loads of uses throughout the home. Its original use was as a laundry detergent booster. Hard water contains minerals that adhere to laundry, appliances, and other surfaces in your home, making cleaning more difficult. These minerals can clog pipes and stain clothes and surfaces, including bathtubs and showers, sinks, washing machines, and dishes. Washing soda softens water by forming a chemical reaction wherein the calcium ions in the washing soda bind to the minerals and wash them away instead of letting them stick to fabrics and surfaces. Softening hard water prevents stains, helps appliances run better, and allows cleaning products to work more effectively. Soft water is also more economical since you can use less soap and detergent to clean and your appliances will last longer when they aren't clogged with mineral buildup. It is often likened to baking soda, but the two ingredients are actually different compounds that can be used in different ways. Perhaps even more confusing is the fact that you can make your own washing soda from baking soda (learn more about this in Chapter 6). Here is some more information about washing soda:

- Washing soda is more abrasive than baking soda and, like baking soda, can scratch delicate surfaces, so it's important to test a small area before using as a scrubbing agent.
- You can find washing soda in most grocery, big-box, and health food stores or online.
- Be sure to handle washing soda with care. As with any highly alkaline substance, undiluted washing soda can damage skin and eyes and is not safe to eat or inhale. Always wear gloves when cleaning with washing soda, and keep it away from kids and pets. However, washing soda is still considered a safe ingredient for natural cleaning and has an A rating for safety from the Environmental Working Group.

Which one should you choose? Check out the following table for guidance.

| Common Uses of Baking Soda versus Washing Soda | |
| --- | --- |
| Baking Soda | Washing Soda |
| Surfaces that can't be thoroughly rinsed, like ovens and floors. | A surface or fabric that won't be damaged by the abrasiveness and can easily be rinsed thoroughly, such as a bathtub. Not for use on fiberglass, tile, or aluminum. |
| Surfaces used for food preparation and areas frequented by children and pets. | Can be used to soften hard water, helping cleaners work more effectively and appliances run more efficiently. |
| Laundry, especially more delicate fabrics. Can be applied directly to fabrics without causing damage. | Laundry, especially sturdy fabrics. Never apply washing soda directly to fabrics, as it may damage the fibers. |

We'll cover baking soda and washing soda in Chapter 6.

## Other Common Natural Ingredients

Aside from baking and washing sodas, the following ingredients are very versatile and will be useful for many cleaning tasks:

○ **All-natural dish soap** is a necessity in any health-conscious home to not only clean dishes without dangerous toxic chemicals, but also as an ingredient found in many recipes throughout this book. You can find natural dish soaps in health food stores and many grocery stores, or make your own with the easy and affordable recipe featured in Chapter 2.

○ **Castile soap** is a natural soap made of vegetable oils. Castile soap is great for using as a natural body wash, shampoo, pet shampoo, and floor cleaner, and it's even great for pest control. It's also touted as a housecleaning soap, laundry soap, dish soap, and more, but I haven't had luck with these applications. Never mix Castile soap with any acid, including white vinegar and lemon. It's not a dangerous combination, but acid "unsaponifies" the soap, which is basically a fancy way of saying it breaks down the soap into its original oils, turning it into a gloppy mess that's useless for cleaning.

○ **Diatomaceous earth**, also called *DE* for short, is a wonderful, safe, and all-natural pest control powder that kills bugs and insects on contact by piercing their exoskeletons, causing them to dehydrate. DE is harmless to mammals but may cause breathing problems in sensitive individuals (like any powder can). Wear a face mask when applying DE, and keep kids and pets away from the area until the dust settles. You can find food-grade diatomaceous earth at pet supply stores and online. Make sure to buy "food-grade," not the toxic "pool-grade," DE.

○ **Distilled water** might be a good option depending on your water source. You don't need to use distilled or filtered water in these DIY cleaning recipes unless your tap water is filled with minerals that may stain or leave a film on surfaces. You can buy distilled water in 1-gallon jugs at the grocery store, or install a water filter on your kitchen sink.

○ **Glass containers** are a more natural option because plastic chemicals won't leach into your natural cleansers. You can purchase new glass cleaning bottles and other containers at health food stores or online, or clean and reuse empty food jars and bottles. To fashion a glass spray bottle for liquid DIY cleaners, take an empty glass bottle (apple cider vinegar bottles are the perfect size for this), and replace the lid with an old spray pump. Now you have a high-quality glass spray bottle that was practically free!

○ **Hydrogen peroxide (3%)** is an excellent germ fighter, so it's a good choice for disinfectants and kitchen and bathroom cleaners. A few important notes: it is toxic when ingested, especially in larger quantities and concentrations; can irritate eyes and skin; and can cause other health problems if absorbed through the skin. However, regular 3% hydrogen peroxide found in drugstores is safe for personal and home care, including disinfecting food surfaces and as a mouthwash (1:1 ratio of hydrogen peroxide and water).

Never mix hydrogen peroxide with vinegar, ammonia, or chlorine bleach because these mixtures may form dangerous gases. As a rule, it's generally a good idea not to mix hydrogen peroxide with any cleaner you plan on storing, in case the mixture may prove unsafe. For example, when hydrogen peroxide is mixed with baking soda and allowed to sit, it not only neutralizes the cleaning power of both ingredients; it can also pose a health and safety hazard. As the mixture sits, it releases carbon dioxide that may make the bottle explode, leak, or spray the cleaner all over when the container is opened. Castile soap is also known to be an unsafe mixture for storage. Hydrogen peroxide is light sensitive and should always be stored in a dark container. Use within 6 months of opening. Unopened bottles will last at least a year. To test whether your hydrogen peroxide is fresh, simply pour some in a glass bowl. If it fizzes, its disinfectant properties are intact.

○ **Sal Suds** is a biodegradable household cleaner made by Dr. Bronner's and is a good choice for basic household cleaning. Note that it is not effective at getting rid of pests.

○ **Salt and oil** (your favorite cooking salt and vegetable oil varieties) can actually be used for some DIY cleaning recipes. Refined coconut oil and olive oil work best for most DIY recipes, but you can use just about any cooking oil you have in your home in a pinch.

○ **Vodka and rubbing (isopropyl) alcohol** are other options. You might see rubbing alcohol more frequently in natural cleaning recipes, but I prefer to use vodka instead since rubbing alcohol is toxic when inhaled or ingested. If you use rubbing alcohol, avoid direct contact with skin, always use in a well-ventilated area, and discontinue use if you experience any symptoms of isopropyl alcohol poisoning, such as headache, dizziness, nausea, vomiting, or breathing problems. Vodka has the same disinfecting properties of rubbing alcohol with a much less offensive scent, and once vodka dries, the scent goes away completely. If you prefer to use rubbing alcohol, feel free to use it instead of vodka in recipes throughout this book, but, of course, always keep it out of reach of children and pets.

○ **White vinegar** is my vinegar of choice for DIY cleaning because it's inexpensive yet still very effective at cleaning dirt and killing germs. You may have seen the 6% acid cleaning vinegar in stores, but that type of vinegar is more expensive and really isn't necessary.

## Essential Oils

One of the most concerning things about commercial cleaners is their use of synthetic fragrances, which almost always contain toxic ingredients that aren't required by law to be listed on the bottle. That doesn't mean that your natural alternatives have to be unscented, though—this is where essential oils come in! Essential oils are an easy and nontoxic way to make your home smell amazing, and some oils even have antibacterial, antifungal, and therapeutic properties and can be used as natural and effective pest repellents.

The use of essential oils in natural cleaning is completely optional. While essential oils do have benefits, all the DIY recipes in this book will work just fine without them.

| Ten Essential Oils Most Commonly Used in Natural Cleaning | |
|---|---|
| Essential Oil | Properties |
| Cinnamon | Antibacterial and antiseptic. |
| Eucalyptus | Germicide. |
| Lavender | Antibacterial and antifungal. |
| Lemon | Germicide. Lemon essential oil can cause photosensitivity when used topically, so avoid direct sunlight and tanning beds for up to 12 hours after using lemon oil on your skin. |
| Orange | Cuts through grease; great for kitchen use. |
| Peppermint | Antibacterial. |
| Pine | Germicide that also kills odors and purifies the air. Common scent used in cleaners. |
| Rosemary | Antibacterial and antiseptic. |
| Tea Tree (Melaleuca) | Germicide. |
| Thyme | Germicide. |

Use essential oils safely: do not ingest essential oils, and be careful using them around children and pets, especially birds and cats. Most of the oils recommended in this book, including lemon, lavender, and tea tree, are safe for children. Peppermint and eucalyptus oils may cause breathing issues in children under 6 years of age. Citrus essential oils, including lemon, lime, orange, grapefruit, and bergamot, can cause photosensitivity in children and adults, which means they can cause skin to be sensitive to UV rays for hours after coming in contact with your skin.

## Know Your Cleaning Properties

You'll see these words throughout the book, so it's good to know exactly what they mean.

| | |
|---|---|
| **Antibacterial** | Kills or hinders the development of bacteria, such as *Listeria monocytogenes*, *Salmonella*, *Staphylococcus aureus*, and *Escherichia coli* (*E. coli*), all of which are known to cause foodborne illnesses. |
| **Antifungal** | Kills fungi, including athlete's foot, ringworm, and candidiasis, commonly known as *thrush*. |
| **Antiseptic** | Cleans disease-causing bacteria, fungi, and viruses from the body. Common antiseptics are hydrogen peroxide, alcohols, and iodine. |
| **Antiviral** | Inhibits the development of viruses, such as colds and influenza. |
| **Disinfectant** | Like antiseptics, disinfectants stop and slow the growth of disease-causing bacteria, fungi, and viruses, but unlike antiseptics, disinfectants are used to clean nonliving surfaces. |
| **Germ** | Any microorganism that can cause illness. The major types of germs include bacteria, fungi, and viruses. |
| **Germicide** | Kills and inhibits the development of bacteria, fungi, and viruses. |

Birds shouldn't be around essential oils at all, and cats are extremely sensitive, as they cannot metabolize certain compounds in essential oils. Even diffusing certain oils around cats can be harmful. If the oil gets on their bodies, they will ingest it when they clean themselves. Essential oils that are known to be toxic to cats include cinnamon, citrus (lemon, grapefruit, orange, etc.), clove, eucalyptus, pennyroyal, peppermint, pine, sweet birch, tea tree (melaleuca), wintergreen, and ylang-ylang, though other essential oils may also be unsafe. Symptoms of poisoning include drooling, vomiting, difficulty walking, tremors, and respiratory issues. If your cat accidentally ingests any essential oils, contact your veterinarian immediately. If you have a cat, it may be best to avoid using any essential oils in your home. Simply omit the oils in the cleaning recipes in this book, or use safe alternatives such as vanilla extract or citrus juices and peels.

Dogs may also be sensitive to certain essential oils. Oils known to be toxic to dogs include cinnamon, citrus, pennyroyal, peppermint, pine, sweet birch, tea tree (melaleuca), wintergreen, and ylang-ylang. The safest oils are cardamom, chamomile, lavender, spearmint, and thyme. Please consult your veterinarian for more guidance on using essential oils around your pets.

## Getting Started

Now that you've gathered your natural cleaning supplies, you're ready to dive right in! You can either read this book straight through or skip to sections to find tips that fit your cleaning needs for the day. Get ready to enjoy a home that is sparkling clean, smells amazing, and is completely free from unhealthy chemical cleaners!

# 2. KITCHENS

The kitchen is one of the busiest rooms in most homes and probably where you do the most cleaning, especially if you cook a lot. Since you handle food here, it's even more important to keep this room extra clean and sanitized so that you and your family will stay safe and healthy. Let these quick and easy tips help you cut through even the toughest grease, dirt, and grime to make your kitchen sparkle—in no time.

# COUNTERTOPS AND CABINETS

Keep food storage and prep areas clean and sanitary with these simple tips.

1 **Clean hard-to-reach areas of dishware and glassware with white rice.** To clean irregularly shaped bottles and other containers, put a handful of rice, water, and a small squirt of dish soap in the container. Cover the container, and shake vigorously. The rice is hard enough and small enough to remove dirt and debris from nooks and crannies inside the container. Dispose of the used rice in the trash can to prevent drain clogs, rinse well, and allow to air-dry.

2 **Remove coffee stains from ceramic mugs with baking soda or salt and lemon.** Sprinkle some baking soda to coat the inside of the mug, and add a little water to form a paste. Use a sponge or cloth to scrub away stains with ease. If baking soda doesn't do the trick, try salt and lemon. Pour a tablespoon each of salt and lemon juice in the bottom of the mug, and add a few ice cubes. Swish around, and watch stains disappear.

**3** **Eliminate silverware scratches from dishes with baking soda.** Make a thick paste with baking soda and a little water. Apply the paste to dishes with a cloth, then scrub. Rinse well, and dry.

**4** **Hand-wash knives to keep them sharp.** It may be tempting to throw your kitchen knives in the dishwasher to let it do all the work, but doing so can dull your knives and promote rust. Hand-wash knives in natural dish soap and warm water to keep them in great shape for years to come. Also, avoid cleaning them with white vinegar or lemon, as acids can cause etching in the steel.

**5** **Deodorize reusable water bottles with baking soda.** Put 2 tablespoons of baking soda in a stinky water bottle, then fill with hot water. Let it sit for 1–2 hours, and wash as usual.

# 6 Save money with a homemade, high-powered dish soap.

Sal Suds alone does a great job when you're hand-washing dishes, but when you're cleaning especially greasy pots and pans, you may need something stronger. This all-natural DIY dish soap gets the job done for a fraction of the price of store-bought, is effective even in hard water, and can also be used when other homemade cleaners throughout this book call for dish soap.

½ cup warm filtered water (minerals in tap water may interfere with thickening)

2 teaspoons kosher or sea salt (used to thicken the soap)

½ cup Sal Suds

½ cup white vinegar

2 teaspoons lemon juice

20–30 drops essential oil (optional; lemon and/or lavender would be good choices)

Squeeze bottle or other storage container

1. Mix the warm water and salt in a medium bowl, and stir until the salt dissolves.
2. In a small bowl, mix the Sal Suds with the vinegar and lemon juice, and stir until combined.

3. Add the soap mixture to the salt mixture, and stir gently to prevent too many bubbles from forming. Stir until the mixture reaches a gel-like consistency.

4. Add your favorite essential oils, if desired. Lemon oil is a great option for additional grease-fighting power, and lavender provides a calming, pleasant smell and antibacterial and antifungal benefits. Do not add essential oils if you used sea salt, because the oils will cause the soap to turn runny again.

5. Pour the dish soap into a squeeze bottle or other container and use within 2–3 months. To use, add a small amount to hot running water, and wash dishes, countertops, and cabinets as usual.

7 **Remove sticky residue from kitchen surfaces with this easy homemade gunk remover.** Mix a 1:1 ratio of coconut oil and baking soda. Make only enough for the job at hand. For instance, if it's a small job, mix 1 tablespoon of each. For larger jobs, start with ½ cup of each. The coconut oil will break down the sticky residue, and baking soda will gently scrub it away.

# 8 Infuse vinegar with citrus, herbs, and spices for better-smelling DIY cleaning recipes.

Some people struggle with natural cleaning because they can't stand the smell of vinegar. Luckily, the smell dissipates once the vinegar dries, but you can also make it smell more pleasant by infusing it with scents!

Your favorite scent combinations, such as mint and lime (mojito, anyone?), orange and clove, or lemon and basil

2½ cups white vinegar

1-quart Mason jar

1. Fill the Mason jar half full with your chosen combination of citrus peels, herbs, and spices.
2. Heat the vinegar to almost boiling. You can heat vinegar in a glass container in the microwave or on the stovetop in a stainless steel or enameled cast iron pot. Do not heat vinegar in aluminum or regular cast iron cookware, since it is reactive with these materials.
3. Fill the jar with the hot vinegar, seal, and let it steep in a dark place at room temperature for at least 24 hours or longer if you want a stronger scent. Strain, and discard the peels, herbs, and spices.
4. Store the vinegar in a cool, dark place, and use diluted, at full strength, or in DIY recipes just as you would regular vinegar.

**9** **Prevent water spots and fingerprints on faucets with waxed paper.** Run the waxy side of waxed paper on your kitchen faucet and other chrome fixtures to help prevent unsightly marks, including water spots and fingerprints. You'll have to re-treat these areas regularly, but they'll look cleaner longer than if you use typical scouring methods.

**10** **Keep your faucet running smoothly with vinegar.** Before you go to bed, pour ¼ to ½ cup of white vinegar into a small plastic food bag, add a few drops of lemon essential oil (if desired for extra cleaning power), and secure the bag onto your faucet with a rubber band or elastic hair tie. The next morning, remove the bag, and wipe your faucet clean. This mixture will remove mineral deposits and soap scum buildup from your faucet and keep it running smoothly.

**11** **Use salt to clean a dropped egg off the floor.** Sprinkle salt on the egg, and let it sit for 30 minutes. You should be able to wipe it up with ease.

**12** **Save money by making your own foaming hand soap refills.** Store-bought soap refills can save you some money over buying new dispensers every time, but making your own homemade hand wash will save you even more! The secret to foaming hand wash is in the pump, not the soap. Keep that empty foaming soap dispenser, and refill it with water and 1 teaspoon of liquid Castile soap or natural dish soap. The pump will work just as it used to!

**13** **Remove stains and odors from hands in a snap with items you already have in your kitchen.** Cutting onions and garlic can make your hands pretty smelly, and washing with regular soap often won't make the odor go away. Clean odors and stains from hands by bathing them in tomato juice, lemon juice, or salt.

**14** **Eliminate fruit flies from your kitchen with apple cider vinegar and sugar.** Fill a small bowl or Mason jar with apple cider vinegar and a spoonful of sugar. Stir to mix, and cover with plastic wrap. Poke some holes in the plastic wrap to allow the flies to access the vinegar mixture without escaping. Once the fruit flies drown in the container, dispose of them in the garbage or outside.

**15** **Soak fresh produce in vinegar to remove wax and pesticides.** For produce with a skin, fill your clean kitchen sink with cool water, and add 1 cup of white vinegar. Add the produce, and let it soak for 20 minutes to an hour. Rinse and dry thoroughly before storing or consuming. Soak more delicate greens, such as lettuce, kale, and spinach, in the vinegar mixture for about 15 minutes, swishing them through the water with your hands to remove dirt and grit, then use a salad spinner to dry thoroughly. Store in a big bowl between layers of paper towels or clean, dry cloths to absorb moisture and keep them fresher longer.

**16** **Clean delicate berries with a homemade all-purpose spray.** Fill a spray bottle with water, and add 2 tablespoons of liquid Castile soap. Screw on the spray nozzle, and shake to combine. Put the berries in a colander, spray liberally with cleaner, and rub berries very gently to keep them from breaking apart. Rinse thoroughly with cool water, and let them sit in the colander for a few minutes to drain the water. Put berries in a storage container lined with paper towels, and store in the fridge. This all-natural spray can be used to clean surfaces throughout your home.

**17** **Use this easy DIY citrus soft scrub to scour kitchen surfaces without scratching.** This mixture will clean and remove stains from sinks, stovetops, and other surfaces without damaging the finish.

1 cup baking soda

¼ cup liquid Castile soap

10 drops each lemon, lime, and orange essential oils

1. Mix the ingredients in a bowl to form a paste. Add more Castile soap if the mixture is too dry.
2. Apply the paste with a microfiber cloth or sponge, scrub, and rinse with clean water.

**18** **Clean and polish your kitchen sink in just a few moments with a lemon and salt.** Cut a lemon in half, dip it in salt, and use it to clean and polish your kitchen sink. The abrasive action of the salt scrubs away stains, while the lemon removes grease, grime, and odors.

**19** **Dissolve hard-water stains around your kitchen with full-strength vinegar.** Soak silverware and glassware in white vinegar, rinse well, and air-dry. Spray your refrigerator's water dispenser with vinegar, wipe with a damp microfiber cloth, and dry with a clean, dry cloth. To clean your kitchen sink, spray with vinegar, and let it sit for 5 minutes. Scrub the sink clean with a sponge or damp microfiber towel, rinse well, and dry. For added cleaning power, soak a cloth in vinegar, and wrap it around the kitchen faucet. Rinse and dry thoroughly.

**20** **Make your own inexpensive, natural, and effective DIY kitchen spray in just minutes.** White vinegar cuts through grease and has antibacterial and antiseptic properties, making it an excellent kitchen cleanser. Fill a spray bottle halfway with white vinegar, then fill it almost to the top with water. Add your favorite antibacterial essential oils (some of which are listed in Chapter 1), using 15 drops per 25 ounces. You can use one essential oil or a combination of two or three scents. Favorite essential oils for kitchen cleaning are lemon, orange, lemongrass, and rosemary, and favorite combinations include lemongrass-basil, lavender-rosemary, tea tree–grapefruit, and lemon-eucalyptus.

## Effective Ways to Clear and Prevent Kitchen Clogs

Before you call a plumber and pay for a repair, try some of these easy hacks to clear out minor drain clogs. Once the drain is clear, use the rest of the ideas to keep things running smoothly going forward.

**21** **Clear clogged or slow-moving drains with a plunger.** Fill the sink half full with warm water, and plunge the drain vigorously using a rubber plunger. Rinse the sink and drain clean with hot water.

**22** **Break up fat, oil, and grease buildup with dish detergent and hot water.** Heat a large pot of water to a boil, then stir in a few tablespoons of natural dish detergent. Pour the near-boiling mixture down the drain, and rinse with hot water. Repeat these steps, as needed, to melt the clog.

**23** **Use soda to break down clogs without damaging pipes.** The acids in regular soda (not diet) are corrosive in nature and can clear drains without damaging your pipes or your skin like standard chemical cleaners can. Pour room temperature soda down the drain, and let it sit for an hour or two. Rinse with hot water.

**24** **Never put fats like cooking oils and grease in the drain or garbage disposal.** Allow fats to cool before throwing away in the garbage.

**25 Wash away grease with salt water.** Salt is abrasive and works as a natural scouring agent. Pour ½ cup of salt down the drain, followed by a pot of boiling water. Rinse with hot water, and repeat, if necessary. Do this once a month to keep drains clear.

**26 Clear tough clogs with a clothes hanger.** Unfold a wire hanger, and make it as straight as you can. Using pliers, bend the end of the wire to form a hook, then use the hook to fish out the clog, being careful not to push the clog down farther into the drain.

**27 Remove hard clogs with a wet/dry vacuum.** Some clogs will be too hard to break down with the methods listed previously. If you have a wet/dry vac, put the vacuum hose on the drain opening, creating the tightest seal possible. With the vacuum on the highest setting, try to suck the clog back up out of the drain.

**28 Dispose of food waste in the garbage or compost bin, not in the garbage disposal.** The garbage disposal can handle small amounts of food debris, but disposing large amounts of food may overload your drain and cause clogs that are difficult to remove. When you have a lot of food waste, such as after peeling potatoes or cutting onions, throw these scraps into the garbage or compost bin instead.

**29** **Keep drains running smoothly and smelling fresh with baking soda.** Sprinkle some baking soda into the drain, then rinse with hot water. Do this once per week, or as often as needed.

**30** **Use vinegar to remove dirt and grime from pipes.** About once a week, pour 1 cup of white vinegar down the drain, and let it sit for 20–30 minutes. Rinse with hot water.

**31** **Deodorize your garbage disposal with leftover citrus peels.** Simply run the water at about half speed, and throw in some orange or lemon peels. Turn on the disposal for about 10 seconds, then let the peels sit for 15–20 minutes to soften any buildup and get rid of smells in your disposal. Turn on the water, and drop in a few ice cubes to blast away dirt and debris. Finally, fill up the sink about halfway with water. Pull the stopper, and run the disposal to flush out the drain.

**32** **Scrub your garbage disposal with an old tooth-brush.** Food particles and other debris can get caught in the folds of the rubber splash guard in your garbage disposal, causing offensive odors that can permeate your kitchen. Lift the splash guard up out of the drain, and scrub with dish soap and a toothbrush to clean grease, food, and odor-causing bacteria. Make sure no one turns on the garbage disposal while you're cleaning it!

**33 Quickly clean your kitchen trash can with cleaning spray.** If you have guests on their way and your trash can smells bad, spray the inside liberally with DIY kitchen spray or another all-purpose spray, and wipe clean with a cloth or paper towels. Spray and wipe the outside of the can, too, if necessary.

**34 Prevent smells from forming in your trash can with baking soda and essential oils.** Keep your trash can fresher longer with this homemade freshening powder. Mix ½ cup of baking soda and 20 drops of your favorite essential oils (optional). Some classic options for the kitchen include lemon, orange, lavender, lemongrass, and eucalyptus. Combine well with a spoon, then sprinkle in the bottom of the trash can (under the trash bag).

**35 Disinfect kitchen surfaces in seconds with hydrogen peroxide.** Put a spray nozzle on a container of hydrogen peroxide or pour it into a dark glass spray bottle, and spray any wiped-down surface to kill any remaining germs. Let it sit for 5 minutes, then wipe dry with a clean cloth. Always store hydrogen peroxide in a dark container since light causes it to decompose much faster. (If you don't have hydrogen peroxide, use vodka!)

# 36 Use a gentle cleanser on soft stone surfaces.

Acids can harm soft stone materials like marble and granite countertops, giving them a dull appearance also known as *etching*. Avoid using white vinegar, lemon, or other acidic materials on or near these surfaces, and instead use this gentle DIY cleanser to clean and disinfect. Fill a spray bottle with warm water, and add 1 tablespoon of gentle, nonabrasive dish soap. Be sure the dish soap does not contain lemon or other acid ingredients. Shake gently to mix. Spray the counter with the solution, wipe with a wet dishcloth, and dry with a soft, absorbent towel.

# 37 Use baking soda to gently scrub scuffs and scratches from laminate countertops.

Pots, pans, and other cookware can leave superficial marks on laminate counters that won't wipe off even with spray cleaner. When this happens, scrub them away with baking soda. Sprinkle some baking soda on the mark, and use a wet rag to scrub the stain without scratching the surface.

# 38 Pick up dust and crumbs inside cabinets with your vacuum.

Use your vacuum's hose attachments to reach into all the corners inside your cabinets, then wipe clean with a damp cloth.

# 39 Make your own all-natural DIY disinfecting wipes.

Keep these wipes on your counter to quickly clean, disinfect, and degrease kitchen surfaces.

1½ cups water

½ cup vodka

3 tablespoons liquid Castile soap or Sal Suds

30 drops lemon essential oil

30 drops tea tree oil

Washcloths or other soft fabric squares

1-quart glass Mason jar (widemouthed jars work best for easy access)

1. Mix the ingredients in a Mason jar or other glass container with a lid. Screw the lid on tight, and shake well to combine.
2. Add as many washcloths as you can fit into the container. You should be able to fit at least 6 regular-sized washcloths. Old cut-up towels and T-shirts also work well. Replace the lid, and shake again to wet the cloths.
3. To use, remove a cloth, wring out the excess cleaning liquid back into the container, and wipe surfaces clean. When the washcloths get dirty, launder with other cleaning towels, and reuse.

**40 Wash and dry walls from top to bottom to prevent streaks.** To clean grease splatters and more from walls, spray liberally with an all-natural, all-purpose cleaner (do a spot test first to ensure paint color doesn't fade). Quickly wipe walls horizontally from top to bottom with a damp microfiber cloth to eliminate streaks from the dripping cleaner, then follow up with a dry cloth to remove any remaining streaks and prevent water damage.

**41 Make wood shine with coconut oil.** Using a clean cloth or paper towels, apply a dab of coconut oil onto wood cabinets and tables to make them shine. Let it sit for 5 minutes, then buff with a clean, dry cloth. Bonus: the lauric acid content in coconut oil also kills germs.

**42 Disinfect sponges to make them last longer.** Fill a bowl with cold water, add 3 tablespoons of salt, and stir to dissolve. Add the sponge, and let it soak overnight. You can also microwave sponges for 2 minutes to kill germs. Just make sure the sponge is wet and does not contain steel or other metals. For an eco-friendlier option, buy sponges that are machine washable, and just pop them in the washing machine every week or two.

**43** **Use cabinet liners to protect cabinets and make them easier to clean.** Line your cabinets with removable liners (not the adhesive kind), and you won't have to deep clean your cupboards as often, if at all. Liners are so much easier to clean. Simply remove them, and wash in warm, soapy water. Allow them to dry completely before putting back in the cabinets.

**44** **Make laminate and ceramic floors sparkle and shine for just a few cents.** Mop floors with a mixture of 1 cup of white vinegar and 1 gallon of water. Add 10–15 drops of essential oil for fragrance, if desired. For tough dirt and stains, pretreat with DIY kitchen spray before mopping as usual.

**45** **Clean scuff marks from vinyl floors with a tennis ball.** Rub scuff marks with a clean tennis ball to remove them instantly.

**46** **Deep clean light fixtures in the dishwasher.** Place glass light covers in the dishwasher to wash away grease and dust easily.

**47 Scrub built-on gunk from cabinets with oil and baking soda.** Form a paste with 1 part coconut oil and 2 parts baking soda to remove grease and grime from cabinets and make them shine in one step! Apply the paste with a sponge, cloth, or toothbrush. Scrub, then wipe clean with a damp microfiber cloth, followed by a clean, dry cloth.

**48 Use bread to pick up glass shards.** If you're in a pinch and don't have something to clean up broken glass, press a piece of bread on the broken glass. The bread will grab the glass and help protect your hands.

**49 Avoid germs by letting sponges dry between uses.** Wet sponges are a breeding ground for bacteria. Always wring them out after use, and store them at the back of your sink or in a sponge holder to dry.

**50 Protect recipe cards with natural hair spray.** Save money on recipe card holders by lightly spraying recipe cards with hair spray to set the ink and prevent food stains. Now you can gently wipe away food messes with ease.

# Natural Ways to Keep Ants Out of the Kitchen

Ants love to invade kitchens, where they can easily find their next meal. Unfortunately, a few ants can quickly become several dozen. Try these easy tricks to evict them for good.

**51** **Make your own all-natural homemade ant bait.**
You really can't stop the ants for good until you get rid of the source: the colony. Mix 1 part borax with 3 parts powdered sugar. Fill small containers, such as bottle caps, with the mixture, and set them out near ant trails. The powdered sugar will attract the ants, and they'll take the powder back to the nest.

**52** **Keep your space clean.** Ants are looking for an easy meal. Cut off their food source, and they'll have to go somewhere else.

**53** **Repel ants with vinegar.** Keep ants off your countertops with a 50/50 solution of white vinegar and water. Just spray and wipe clean. Ants dislike the smell of vinegar, so they'll stay away.

**54** **Use peppermint oil to send ants packing.** Ants also dislike peppermint oil. Put several drops of peppermint oil on cotton balls, and place them wherever you find ants in your home. Be sure to keep them out of reach of small children and pets.

**55** **Keep ants out with citrus peels.** Place fresh citrus slices or dried peels near entrance points. Ants don't like the smell of citrus and won't enter your home.

**56** **Use diatomaceous earth for an easy way to get rid of carpenter ants.** Carpenter ants don't carry food back to their nests, so their treatment is a little more difficult. They nest in wood and build tunnels through it, so you may find them living in your foundation, deck, or woodpiles near your home. To get rid of the carpenter ants, sprinkle some food-grade diatomaceous earth directly into their nest, making sure to get the powder into all the cracks and crevices.

**57** **Spray the nest.** If you're lucky enough to actually find the nest, give it a good, soaking spray. Any natural cleansing spray will do because you're basically drowning the nest's inhabitants. How do you find the nest? Follow the ant path.

**58** **Seal up cracks and crevices in your home to keep ants from getting inside.** Use caulk to seal openings around doors and windows. This can also save you money on energy bills.

**59** **Be vigilant.** The best way to get rid of ants in your home is to keep at it. They're pretty resourceful little buggers (pun intended), but if you keep after them, you'll eventually win.

# REFRIGERATORS AND OTHER APPLIANCES

Cleaning electronic appliances the right way can make them work better, last longer, and run more efficiently, saving you money on energy bills.

**6O Make a simple, inexpensive homemade stainless steel cleaner.** Fill a spray bottle with ½ water and ½ white vinegar, and mix together. Spray stainless steel fixtures and appliances with the solution, and wipe clean (with the grain—wiping stainless steel in circular motions can cause streaks) with a microfiber cloth or paper towels.

**61 Polish stainless steel with olive oil.** Use olive oil to remove water spots and fingerprints from stainless steel surfaces. Apply a nickel-sized amount of olive oil on a paper towel, and wipe with the grain, left to right. Wipe the entire appliance in long, sweeping motions along the grain, then buff with a microfiber cloth to remove excess oil and make it shine.

# Quick Ways to Deep Clean Your Refrigerator

Instead of feeling overwhelmed at the thought of emptying your fridge to give it a thorough cleaning, use these tips to get the chore done in a flash!

**62 Clean one section at a time.** If you plan to clean the whole fridge at once, start at the top, and work down. If you prefer to remove all your food to clean, store perishables in a cooler with ice to keep them fresh and cool while you work. If you have only a few minutes, just clean one shelf or section a day.

**63 Pretreat sticky surfaces.** Spray sticky, grimy surfaces with all-purpose spray. For dried-on spills, place a wet microfiber cloth on the area. Let it sit for a few minutes, and wipe clean.

**64 Disinfect raw meat and poultry messes.** When cleaning spills from raw meat or poultry, wipe up the spill, then clean the area with hot water. Disinfect with a spray of hydrogen peroxide. Let it sit for 5 minutes, and wipe dry.

**65 Remove shelves and drawers to clean them more thoroughly.** Take out all removable components, and hand-wash with warm, soapy water. Dry well before putting them back in the fridge.

**66** **Remove the vent cover on the bottom of the fridge, and clean in warm, soapy water.** Dry well, and replace. Vacuum under and behind the fridge, using attachments to clean in cracks and crevices. Keeping these areas clean will help your fridge run more efficiently and last longer. Replace the vent cover once it's completely dry.

**67** **Check the drip pan.** Some refrigerators have a removable drip pan underneath to collect condensation. If your fridge has a drip pan, you'll find it behind the grille above the condenser coils. Remove the drip pan, clean with soap and water, and dry well before replacing.

**68** **Clean hard-to-reach areas with cotton swabs.** As you run a damp microfiber cloth in all the cracks and crevices around door seals and handles, keep an eye out for any areas you can't access properly. Use cotton swabs to reach those spots.

**69** **Dry the interior thoroughly with a microfiber cloth.** Use a clean, dry cloth to completely dry the refrigerator shelves to prevent dust from sticking to moist surfaces.

**70** **Put paper towels or cloths in the bottom of crisper drawers.** Store large, sturdy produce, such as celery, peppers, and fruit, in crisper drawers lined with dry kitchen cloths or paper towels to remove moisture and help prevent spoiling. Replace towels weekly.

## 71 Keep your fridge smelling fresh with a home-made deodorizer.

2 cups baking soda

20–30 drops lemon essential oil

1-pint Mason jar or baking soda box

1. Mix the baking soda and essential oil in a 1-pint Mason jar or baking soda box. Start with 20 drops of the essential oil, and add more as needed.
2. Store the mixture uncovered in the refrigerator to freshen and absorb odors. Each batch should last approximately 1–2 months.

## 72 Make your home smell great without toxic synthetic fragrances. Boil a small pot of water, and add some sweet-smelling fragrances such as a few drops of vanilla extract or essential oil, cinnamon sticks, and orange peels to freshen your home naturally.

# 73 Deep clean your oven without harsh chemicals.

Remove even the toughest baked-on food without hard scrubbing with this DIY scouring paste.

½ cup baking soda

¼ cup hydrogen peroxide

¼ cup liquid dish soap

1 tablespoon white vinegar

1 tablespoon lemon juice

Scrub sponge and cleaning cloths or paper towels

1. First, wipe down the oven with warm, soapy water. Use a scrub sponge to clean away easy-to-remove dirt and debris.

2. Next, mix the ingredients in a bowl to form a thick paste, and apply the cleaning solution to baked-on grease and grime inside your oven. Let it sit for 1–2 hours, then wipe clean with a sponge. Continuously dip the sponge in the soapy water to keep it clean as you wipe out the oven.

3. Once all the grime is scrubbed away, make a final wipe with a clean, damp cloth or paper towels, followed by clean, dry cloths.

**74** **Clean oven racks in your bathtub.** Since oven racks are so big, it's difficult to soak them in the sink to remove baked-on messes. Take them to the bathtub, where you can soak and clean the entire racks at once, which will save you loads of time and effort! Carefully put the racks in the bathtub, and sprinkle liberally with baking soda. Spray with water until the baking soda forms a thick paste, then let them sit for about 20 minutes. Scrub them with a sponge, and rinse clean. Air-dry the racks completely before putting them back in the oven.

**75** **Use washing soda to remove burned-on food from burner pans.** Add ½ cup of washing soda to 1 gallon of hot water. Soak burner pans for at least 30 minutes. For really stubborn grease, sprinkle washing soda on a sponge, and scrub it directly on the grease.

**76** **Wipe off greasy buildup from your stovetop and range hood with cooking oil.** Rub a dab of olive oil or coconut oil over greasy surfaces to quickly loosen grease and grime, then wipe clean with kitchen spray and a cloth. This method removes sticky, oily buildup much easier than using soap!

77 **Clean stove burners safely and quickly.** Allow burners to cool completely before cleaning. Remove the burners from the stovetop, and use a cloth dipped in warm, soapy water to wipe away grease and light messes from burner coils. Be careful not to get any electrical components wet, and never submerge burners in water or other liquids. For tougher messes, make a paste with a 2:1 ratio of baking soda and water. Apply the paste to the burner, let it sit for 10 minutes, then wipe away residue.

78 **Use baking soda as a scrub-free stovetop cleaner.** Sprinkle cooked-on messes with baking soda, and spray with water or DIY kitchen spray. Let it sit for about 30 minutes, then wipe clean. Stains should lift right up. Repeat on stubborn messes.

79 **Clean oven spills with salt.** If food boils over in your oven, immediately sprinkle it with salt. Once the oven cools, you can easily wipe up the mess.

**80** **Boil your range hood filter to melt away dirt and grease effortlessly.** Take a pot big enough to hold at least half of your filter, fill it with water, and bring it to a boil. Add ½ cup of baking soda very slowly to keep it from fizzing. Add your filter, and boil it for about 5 minutes or until the grease loosens from the filter. Depending on how large your filter is, you may have to boil half of it at a time. Remove the filter from the pot, and rinse under hot water until the water runs clean. Repeat if the filter is still greasy. Prop up the filter to air-dry, then place it back in the range hood.

**81** **Deodorize your dishwasher with vinegar.** Put one or two small bowls right-side up on the top rack of the dishwasher. Fill the bowls with white vinegar, and run dishwasher as usual with no other dishes in it. To remove soap scum, wipe with a scrub sponge or microfiber cloth immediately after the cycle ends. The hot water will have loosened buildup, making it much easier to clean.

**82** **Turn on your blender to clean tough messes easily.** Fill your blender with warm, soapy water, and turn it on to clean without scrubbing. Rinse well, then air-dry.

# 83 Save time and money with homemade dishwasher tablets.

**Save time and money with homemade dishwasher tablets.** These DIY dishwasher tablets are easy on your wallet and will help you save time with grab-and-go convenience. If you prefer to use dishwasher powder, simply omit the water, and add 1 tablespoon of powder to every load.

1 cup baking soda

1 cup washing soda

1 cup kosher salt

½ cup citric acid (a powder available at the grocery store in the canning aisle, at health food stores, or online)

½ cup to 1 cup water

40–50 drops essential oil (optional; consider lemon, orange, and lemongrass)

Ice cube trays or square silicon molds

1. In a glass or stainless steel bowl, mix the dry ingredients together. Add the water gradually, starting with ½ cup, waiting for the fizzing to die down before adding more to form a dry paste. Stir very well to combine. Add a little more water if the powder is still too crumbly to stick together.
2. Add your favorite essential oils, if desired, for fragrance and a little extra cleaning power.

**3** Spoon the mixture into each compartment of an ice cube tray or square silicon mold, and press firmly into the tray to form a tablet. Try to use ice cube trays that will make tablets small enough to fit in your dishwasher's soap dispenser. This recipe makes approximately 20–24 tablets, depending on the size of the ice cube tray, so you'll probably need two trays.

**4** To use, put one tablet in the dispenser, and run the wash cycle as usual. If the tablet is too large, just toss it on the top rack of your dishwasher.

**84** **Prevent messes in your toaster oven with aluminum foil.** Line your toaster tray with foil, so you'll have to replace only the foil instead of scrubbing cooked-on messes.

**85** **Scrub the dishwasher filter with a toothbrush to keep it functional and extend the life of your dishwasher.** Remove the bottom rack from your dishwasher to access the filter on the floor of the unit. Remove the filter, and wipe off larger food particles into the trash can with a paper towel or cloth. Wash the filter in soapy water, and scrub gently with a toothbrush to remove stuck-on food. Do this once a month to keep your dishwasher in top condition.

**86** **Steam clean your microwave to remove stuck-on foods effortlessly.** Mix 2 cups of water and 2 tablespoons of white vinegar in a microwave-safe bowl. Add a few drops of essential oil to mask the vinegar smell, if desired. Microwave on high for 5 minutes, and let it sit another 2–3 minutes to allow the steam to work. Wipe clean with a microfiber cloth or sponge. The dirt and food should come off easily.

**87** **Remove coffee bean oils from your coffee grinder with rice.** Grind a handful of uncooked white rice in your coffee grinder. Repeat, if necessary, then wipe clean with a microfiber cloth or paper towels. Don't want to use up your rice? You can also use soft white bread for this job.

**88** **Brush away toaster crumbs with a paintbrush.** To clean the toaster, unplug it for safety, then remove the crumb tray. Empty the crumb tray in the trash, and set aside. Turn the toaster upside down over the trash can to dislodge the crumbs inside. Use a clean, dry paintbrush to brush away any remaining crumbs. Clean the outside of the toaster with soapy water and a microfiber cloth or toothbrush, taking care not to get the appliance too wet to harm electrical components. Wipe clean with a damp microfiber cloth, and polish the outside with some white vinegar on a clean cloth to make it shine.

**89** **Deep clean your coffee maker with vinegar.** Fill the water chamber with equal parts white vinegar and water, and run the machine until all the liquid goes through. Repeat at least 2 more times with plain water. Make sure the taste of vinegar is completely gone from the machine before using normally. Wash your coffee maker at least once a month to ensure your coffee tastes fresh. You can use this method to clean your Keurig coffee maker too!

## Tips for Cleaning and Organizing Your Pantry

Most people store the bulk of their food in the pantry, but since the space is often hidden, you might not clean it as often as you should. At best, this can make your pantry a messy, disorganized space that makes it difficult to quickly find what you need, but at worst, it can actually have a negative effect on sanitation and food safety. Learn how to clean your pantry the easy way with these smart tips.

90 **Take everything out of the pantry when you want to deep clean it.** Remove all the food and cookware from your pantry, and thoroughly wipe down shelves with a microfiber cloth dipped in warm, soapy water. If your shelves aren't very soiled, you can just use a damp microfiber cloth and some DIY kitchen spray for especially dirty spots. Take out removable shelves; soak and wash them in the kitchen sink in warm, soapy water; rinse well; and dry completely. Vacuum the floor of the pantry, and use the crevice tool to vacuum in corners and other tight spots.

91 **Throw away spoiled and expired food.** Put any leaky foods in sturdy new containers to prevent future messes.

92 **Wipe off containers.** Clean any dusty or greasy containers with a damp cloth, and dry before replacing in the pantry.

**93** **Keep dry goods fresher longer by storing in hard plastic and glass containers.** Did you know that pantry moths can chew right through paper, thin plastic, and cardboard packaging to access your food? Keep all your dry goods, including cereals, flour, sugar, rice, bread crumbs, crackers, and more, in airtight containers to keep them fresher longer and prevent pests like ants, houseflies, and pantry moths from contaminating your food. If space is tight, try stackable containers.

**94** **Label everything.** Prevent waste by clearly labeling and dating your food. That way, you'll know when it's set to expire so you can use it beforehand.

**95** **Organize your pantry.** As you put food back in your pantry, take the time to organize your space. Store similar items together, label and date containers, and keep your favorites where they can be easily accessed.

**96** **Keep it up.** You should deep clean your pantry and other storage areas at least 3–4 times per year, and perform more routine maintenance—such as cleaning the floor, discarding spoiled food, and wiping up spills and other big messes—every time you clean or at least once a month.

# POTS, PANS, AND MORE

**97** **Quickly remove grease from cookware with baking soda and lemon juice.** Soak pots, pans, cookie sheets, and baking dishes in a sink filled with hot water, ½ cup of baking soda, and ¼ cup of lemon juice. Let them sit 10–15 minutes, wipe, and then rinse clean.

**98** **Extend the life of nonstick pans by hand-washing them.** Washing nonstick pans in the dishwasher can break down the nonstick coating over time. Hand-washing pans in natural dish soap and warm water will keep the coating intact for much longer. Avoid using harsh scrubbers that can also damage nonstick surfaces.

**99** **Make copper cookware shine like new with ketchup.** Rub a generous dab of ketchup all over the pan. Let it sit for 10 minutes. Then wash and rinse clean. Ketchup's thick consistency allows it to stick to surfaces, and its acid and salt content removes tarnish and stains quickly and easily for efficient cleaning.

**100** **Remove limescale from a teakettle with vinegar.** Add ½ cup of white vinegar to a kettle, and fill with water. Let it sit overnight, then boil the kettle. Empty the contents and watch flakes of limescale flow down the drain. Fill the kettle with water, boil again, and empty. The kettle is now ready for use.

**101** **Remove stains from enamel pans with rhubarb.** Put a handful of rhubarb leaves in the pan with some water, and simmer for 10 minutes. Let it sit for around an hour, and then wash as usual. The oxalic acid naturally found in rhubarb leaves will remove even burned-on foods much faster than soaking.

**102** **Use lemon to make cookware shine.** Rub half a lemon or a sprinkle of lemon juice on metal cookware, rinse, and air-dry.

**103** **Polish silver with cornstarch.** Make a thick paste with cornstarch and water. Rub silver with paste, and rinse thoroughly. Don't have cornstarch in the house? You can also use plain white toothpaste!

# Simple Ways to Care for Cast Iron Pans

There's a reason why cast iron cookware is passed down through generations. A well-seasoned cast iron pan is one of the best nonstick surfaces around, doesn't contain all those nasty chemicals found in many contemporary nonstick pans, and actually adds healthy iron to your foods. With proper care, these pans can last a lifetime—or even longer!

**104** **Avoid washing cast iron with soap, and never let it soak.** The only time you may want to use soap to clean your pan is when you first buy it. The rest of the time, you should avoid using dish soap to wash cast iron because it may remove the nonstick seasoning. Cooking foods at high temperatures will kill any bacteria left behind. To clean cast iron, you usually need to only wipe it out with a dry cloth or paper towels. If you cooked something messy, rinse it out with hot water, wipe with a sponge or washcloth, then dry completely before storing.

**105** **Wash pans while they're still warm.** It may be tempting to leave the dishes until morning, but cleaning pots and pans is easiest when they're warm. If you're still having trouble with baked-on and burned-on messes, add some water to the pan, and boil it on the stove for a few minutes to loosen even the toughest messes in no time!

# 106 Season it before its first use. Some cast iron pans sold in stores today come preseasoned and ready to use, but it's still a good idea to know how to do this since you may need to season your pan throughout its lifetime to keep its nonstick surface in good shape.

Dish soap

Nonmetallic sponge, washcloth, or stiff brush

Clean, dry cloth towels or paper towels

Vegetable oil

Aluminum foil

1 Preheat your oven to 350°F. Wash your new pan in hot, soapy water using a nonmetallic sponge, washcloth, or brush, then rinse and dry thoroughly with clean, dry cloth towels or paper towels.

2 Put a small drop of vegetable oil into the pan, and rub the oil all over the surface of the pan, including the exterior.

3 Put the pan upside down directly on the center rack in the oven, place a sheet of aluminum foil on the rack below to catch any oil drips, and bake the pan for 1 hour. Turn off the oven, and let the pan cool completely before removing. Now your pan is ready to use! Repeat this process anytime you notice food sticking to your cookware.

**107** **Use salt to scrub away stuck-on food.** To scrub stuck-on food without removing the seasoning from the pan, sprinkle some kosher salt in the pan. Add a few drops of water to form a paste, and use your fingers or a cloth to scrub away the stuck-on residue.

**108** **Be careful when cooking acidic foods in your cast iron cookware.** Acidic foods like tomatoes, citrus juices, and wine can damage the nonstick seasoning on your pan and may give food a metallic taste. If your pan is well seasoned, you shouldn't have a problem, but if your pan is newer or not in the best shape, it's wise to wait to cook acidic foods in it until you can build a better seasoning on the pan's surface.

**109** **Completely dry cast iron before storing.** Cast iron pans must be stored in completely dry conditions to prevent them from rusting. Dry wet pans with paper towels or a clean dry cloth, or put a freshly washed pan back on a hot burner until dry. Place paper towels between nested pans to soak up any moisture that may crop up during storage.

**110** **Protect pans with cooking oil.** After washing and drying a cast iron pan, place a drop of cooking oil inside the pan to help keep the seasoning in good shape. Rub the oil into the pan with a paper towel. Let it sit for 5 minutes before wiping the excess oil out of the pan with a clean, dry paper towel, then store.

**111** **Make a rusty cast iron skillet like new again with steel wool.** Restore a rusty pan with this easy DIY method. Scrub the rust with a steel wool scrubber until it's completely gone, then wash the pan thoroughly in warm, soapy water, using a scrub brush or sponge. Thoroughly dry the skillet with a clean, dry cloth or paper towels, and re-season the pan.

**112** **Remove rust with a potato.** Having trouble removing that rust? Try a potato! Potatoes naturally contain oxalic acid, an ingredient in many household cleaning products that dissolves rust. Cut a potato in half, pour kosher salt into the pan, and use the salt and cut side of the potato as a scrubber. Once the rust is removed, rinse the pan, dry thoroughly, and re-season.

**113** **Avoid using metal cooking utensils.** Use gentler utensils like silicone, rubber, and wood instead of metal to keep the seasoning intact. Occasional metal spatula usage is okay, but using these gentler tools will make building and maintaining the seasoning so much easier.

**114** **Use cream of tartar to loosen tough, burned-on messes.** Burned-on food is one of the toughest messes to clean! Bring 1 cup of water and 2 tablespoons of cream of tartar to a boil in the messy pot or pan. Let it sit on the stovetop until cool, then wash with dish soap and water. The abrasive consistency and acid content in cream of tartar crystals make it effective at cleaning and polishing even the messiest pots and pans.

**115** **Remove burned-on foods with ketchup.** If you want to use a more hands-off approach, try this method. Pour a thick layer of ketchup to coat the burned mess, and let it sit overnight. The next morning, wipe the pan clean in soapy water. The acids in the tomatoes and vinegar in the ketchup will eat away at stuck-on messes while you sleep.

**116** **Clean baked-on stains from pans with baking soda and hydrogen peroxide.** Sprinkle baking soda on the pan, then spray enough hydrogen peroxide to wet the baking soda and make it foam. Add another layer of baking soda, and let it sit for at least a couple hours or overnight. Wipe the pan clean with a cloth or scrub sponge—no hard scrubbing required! Repeat this process as many times as needed to get the pan completely clean, then wash, dry immediately, and store.

**117** **Nix stains and tarnish from silverware in no time with baking soda and hydrogen peroxide.** Pour 1 cup of baking soda into a small bowl, and add enough hydrogen peroxide to form a thick paste. (You can start with more or less baking soda, depending on how many pieces of silverware you're cleaning.) Put on protective gloves, apply the paste to the silverware, then rub dirt and tarnish away with your hands, a cloth, or a scrub sponge. Once the stains and tarnish are removed, hand-wash the silverware, or pop them in the dishwasher.

**118** **Clean stuck-on cheese from your grater with a potato.** Grate a raw potato with your grater to remove dried cheese from all the little cracks and crevices.

**119** **Restore tarnished silver with a hands-off mixture of baking soda, salt, and aluminum foil.** Place silver in a bowl lined with aluminum foil. Add 1 cup each of baking soda and kosher salt, then fill the bowl with enough hot water to cover the silver at least partially (for larger pieces, you may have to work in stages, depending on the size of your bowl). Soak the silver for 5 minutes, then hand-wash and polish as usual.

# Natural Ways to Clean and Protect Cutting Boards

Cleaning wooden cutting boards with water and dish detergent can weaken the wood, and small cuts and scratches are perfect places for bacteria to hide even after washing. Follow these hacks to ensure your wooden and plastic cutting boards stay clean and beautiful for years to come.

**120** **Make your own cleaning scrub.** Periodically deep clean your cutting boards by scrubbing with a thick paste made from 1 tablespoon each of baking soda, salt, and water. Rinse thoroughly with hot water. This cleaning method will also remove light stains.

**121** **Disinfect with vinegar.** To disinfect and clean wooden and plastic cutting boards, wipe them with a paper towel drenched in full-strength white vinegar after each use.

**122** **Clean your grill with salt and lemon.** Cut a lemon in half, and dip the cut side in salt. Kosher salt works great for this since the granules are larger and, therefore, more abrasive. Using a grill fork or tongs to hold the lemon, rub the cut side over hot grill grates, applying more pressure to remove buildup. Replace the lemon as needed. Let the grill cool completely, then rinse the grate with clean water from the hose. Dry with paper towels, or replace on the grill and heat until dry to prevent rusting.

**123** **Deodorize with baking soda.** Some foods, such as garlic and onions, can leave offensive odors behind. When your cutting board needs deodorizing, sprinkle liberally with baking soda, and spray with white vinegar until bubbles form. Let it bubble for 10 minutes. Rinse, dry, and store.

**124** **Remove odors with lemon.** You can also use half of a cut lemon or bottled lemon juice to neutralize odors and help sanitize. Rub the board with the cut side of a lemon or a generous splash of bottled lemon juice. Rinse, dry, and store.

**125** **Use lemon essential oil to remove stains.** Add 5–10 drops of lemon essential oil to ¼ cup of water. Pour the mixture onto a sponge, and use the saturated sponge to wipe the lemon solution on the cutting board. Set the board out in the sun, and repeat the process until the stain is gone.

**126** **Remove really tough buildup from your grill with washing soda.** If your grill is in really bad shape, you may need a more powerful cleaner. Fill a storage bin or bathtub with enough water to cover the grill grates. Sprinkle liberally with washing soda, and stir with a gloved hand to mix. Soak the grates in the mixture for about 10–15 minutes, then scrub with a grill brush until clean.

# 3. LIVING AREAS

Knowing how to clean and maintain your carpets, hardwood floors, furniture, and electronics can keep them looking like new, help them last longer, and save you tons of money in the long run.

**127** **Clean light bulbs with vodka.** Periodically cleaning your light bulbs can really brighten up a room! Moisten a cleaning cloth with vodka, and use it to wipe dust buildup from light bulbs.

**128** **Vacuum dining room chairs to clean dirt and pet hair with ease.** Use your vacuum's upholstery attachment to clean between wood spindles and in upholstery creases on dining room chairs. Do this before you clean the floor so that debris missed by the vacuum can fall below and get cleaned up later.

**129** **Immediately blot fresh food spills on upholstered dining chairs to prevent staining.** To keep spilled foods from staining upholstery, it's important to act quickly. As soon as possible, start blotting the stain with a cloth or paper towels, and use one of the carpet stain removal recipes in the next section, if necessary.

**130** **Learn to read furniture tags to find out the best cleaning method for your upholstered furniture or dining set.** All dining room chairs have a tag that lists the recommended cleaning method. A "W" on the tag means a water-based cleaning product may be used, but an "S" means you should avoid cleaning with water. Some tags will have both letters, which means either method is fine. "X" means the chairs should be professionally cleaned. Even if you know the recommended cleaning method, you should still test any DIY recipes on an inconspicuous area of the fabric to ensure safety and colorfastness.

**131** **Silence squeaky hinges with cooking oil.** Use your finger to apply a dab of your favorite cooking oil on a squeaky hinge. Open and shut the door several times to work the oil into the hinge, then wipe away the excess oil with a cloth or paper towel.

# 132 Protect wood furniture with DIY orange oil spray.

This homemade orange oil wood polish will make your wood shine like new!

½ cup white vinegar

1 cup olive oil

Peel and zest of 1 orange (optional)

20 drops orange essential oil

Spray bottle

1. Heat the vinegar, olive oil, and orange peel and zest in a medium saucepan over medium-high heat until hot but not yet boiling. Remove the pan from the heat, and let it sit for several hours or overnight to release the natural oils in the orange peel.

2. Once the mixture is completely cooled, strain it into a measuring cup, discard the peels, and pour the liquid into a spray bottle. Add the orange essential oil, and shake to combine. If you're not using the orange peel, just mix the vinegar, olive oil, and orange essential oil, and shake to combine.

3. To use, shake to combine the ingredients, and test in an inconspicuous spot. Spray on a cloth or directly on wood furniture. Polish furniture with a cloth, and let the polish sit for 10 minutes before wiping again with a clean, dry cloth to remove excess oil.

## Tried-and-True Natural Ways to Remove Food Stains from Carpeting

If your dining room is carpeted, food messes can be a real pain. These stain removal hacks will make your carpet look good as new. Use white cloths and paper towels to prevent ink and color transfer onto the carpet you're trying to clean.

**133** **Absorb liquid spills with cornstarch.** Clean up as much liquid as you can with white cloths or paper towels. Sprinkle the stain liberally with cornstarch, and let it sit for 30 minutes to an hour until the cornstarch absorbs the liquid. Sweep up any excess powder you can with a broom and dustpan, then vacuum. If the carpet is still stained, treat with plain, unflavored club soda, and blot until the stain comes out.

**134** **Treat juice, grease, and oil stains with shaving cream.** For juice spills, blot the liquid, and apply some shaving cream. Use a damp sponge or cloth to wipe clean. For grease and oil, apply the shaving cream, and work it into the stain. Let it dry, then rub clean with a cloth. The soap and acids in shaving cream break down and lift stains away in no time.

**135 Remove coffee and tea stains with beer.** To clean up coffee and tea spills, first soak up as much liquid as you can with cloths or paper towels, then pour some room temperature beer on the stain. Lightly blot the beer into the carpet, and watch as the stain disappears! The carbonation and acid content in beer make it an excellent stain fighter. You may have to repeat the process to fully remove all traces of the stain. Once the stain lifts, rinse away the beer and remaining residue with clean water, then blot or use a wet/dry vac to dry.

**136 Freeze away gum with ice.** Use an ice cube to freeze gum embedded in carpets, then scrape it out with a paring knife. This method works on melted wax too!

**137 Get rid of fruit and juice stains with laundry detergent and vinegar.** Mix 2 cups of water with 1 tablespoon of laundry detergent and 1½ tablespoons of white vinegar. Soak up the bulk of the spill with paper towels or dry cloths. Apply the cleaning solution to the stain, and blot to remove.

**138 Clean red wine stains with white wine and salt.** Clean up as much liquid as possible with paper towels or a dry cloth. While the red wine is still wet, pour white wine or another clear liquor, such as vodka, over the stain to dilute the color. Clean the stain with a cloth or sponge and cold water, then pour salt on the stain. Let it sit for around 10 minutes, then vacuum it up.

**139** **Lift oil stains with salt and vodka.** Combine 4 parts vodka to 1 part salt, and rub the mixture into the stain until removed.

**140** **Nix ketchup stains with salt.** Pour salt over the ketchup spill, and let it sit for 10 minutes. Vacuum, and wipe clean with a damp cloth or sponge. Repeat the process as often as needed to lift the stain.

**141** **Use club soda for grease, red wine, and other colorful drinks.** Remove as much liquid from the carpet as possible with paper towels or cloths, then douse the stain with a little plain, unflavored club soda. Use cloths or paper towels to blot the stain away.

**142** **Absorb oil stains with baking soda and dish soap.** Sprinkle the stain with baking soda, and rub it gently into the carpet. Let it sit for 30 minutes, then vacuum it up. Add a dab of dish soap to the stain, and rub it into the carpet using your fingers or a toothbrush. Pour a little warm water over the stain, and start blotting with a cloth until the stain lifts out of the carpet.

## 143 Dust first, then clean floors. It's best to work with gravity when cleaning so you won't have to clean anything more than once. Work from top to bottom in every room. Clean ceiling fans first; then walls, windows, and furniture; and finish up with floors last.

## 144 Place doormats inside and outside all entrances. You will drastically reduce tracked-in dirt by keeping doormats on both sides of all outside doors.

## 145 Clean dust and dirt with the damp-duster method. You really don't need to disinfect most areas in your home, so you don't even need to use cleaning spray. The friction from wiping surfaces with a microfiber cloth is more than enough to kill most germs. Simply wet a microfiber cloth with warm or hot water, and wring it as dry as you can. Wipe surfaces to remove dust and dirt, and follow up with a clean, dry cloth when dusting wood surfaces. You may need a mild DIY cleaning spray to remove tough, stuck-on messes, but for day-to-day cleaning, water and a microfiber cloth should do the trick.

**146** **Remove dust and pet hair from lampshades and speakers with a lint roller.** Instead of pushing the hair around, grab it with the sticky lint roller.

**147** **Dust candles with pantyhose.** Cleaning cloths just push dust into candles, making them look even dirtier than they did before. Use pantyhose or knee-highs to remove dust from candles quickly and easily.

**148** **Wash knickknacks (even candles!) in warm, soapy water.** Once or twice a year, hand-wash your knickknacks like you do your dishes to remove dust buildup. You can use this method on candles to make them look new again! Don't worry; they'll burn just as well as they did before once they air-dry.

**149** **Use a covered broom to clean the walls.** Put a clean cloth over the bristles of a broom to reach cobwebs and dust near ceilings.

# 150 Use the dishwasher to clean and disinfect kids'
**toys.** Pop your children's plastic toys in the dishwasher
to keep them clean. Do this regularly, especially during
cold and flu seasons. While you're at it, throw in other
non-food-based items, like glass light covers, vent hood
filters, and AC vent covers.

# 151 Wipe down the walls with a microfiber mop.
Spray the wall with all-purpose cleaner, then wipe clean
with a clean microfiber mop to reach from floor to ceiling without bending or using a stepladder. Don't have
a microfiber mop? Just drape a damp microfiber cloth
around a dry mop.

# 152 Remove crayon from walls with mayonnaise.
Put a layer of mayo on the crayon stain, and let it sit for
20–30 minutes. Wipe away with a cloth or paper towels.
The oils in the mayo will break down the crayon wax, so
you can wipe the stain away with ease. You can also use
plain white toothpaste for smaller areas.

**153** **Dust ceiling fans with a pillowcase.** Put a pillowcase over a ceiling fan blade, and carefully trap dirt and dust inside as you remove it. Repeat for the other blades. This method prevents dust and debris from falling to the floor and making a bigger mess. When finished, shake the dirt from the pillowcase into the garbage, and launder as usual.

**154** **Prevent scuff marks on baseboards with tape.** Put packing or masking tape on the corners of your vacuum so it won't leave marks when you accidentally run into baseboards.

**155** **Disinfect doorknobs with a spritz of hydrogen peroxide.** Doorknobs are often forgotten when cleaning yet are one of the leading spots for germs and viruses to be passed among family members. Keep them clean, shiny, and free from germs with a little spray of hydrogen peroxide, followed by a quick wipe with a microfiber cloth. Do this at least once a week and every day during cold and flu seasons to help keep your family healthy. You can also use vodka if you prefer.

**156** **Keep throw rugs in place with bathroom sealant.**
Apply acrylic sealant (typically used to seal tubs, sinks, and showers) to the bottom of your throw rugs to keep them from moving around on bare floors. Allow the sealant to dry completely before replacing the rugs on the floor.

**157** **Use an extension cord to vacuum faster.**
Save time and effort finding a new outlet for every room by plugging in your vacuum with an extension cord. A 50-foot cord works great in most homes.

**158** **Clean popcorn ceilings with your vacuum's brush attachment.** Use the brush attachment on your vacuum to dust and remove cobwebs from popcorn ceilings without damaging the plaster like most cleaning methods can.

**159** **Transform a chenille sock into a reusable dry mop cloth.** Slip a large, stretchy sock over your dry mop, then throw it in the washer when you're done cleaning.

**160** **Wipe glue from a hot glue gun with aluminum foil.** The next time you break out the crafts, keep this smart tip in mind. Using a paper towel to wipe glue from a hot glue gun (or any glue bottle, for that matter) can make a huge mess when the paper towel sticks to the glue. Instead, use aluminum foil to wipe away glue without the mess!

**161** **Pick up glitter with clay.** Brooms and vacuums can seem to just push glitter around—instead, press kids' clay on the glitter. The glitter will immediately stick to the clay, and your kids can still play with the clay!

**162** **Use a floor steamer to clean and disinfect without chemicals.** Steam cleaners clean and disinfect tile, laminate, and carpet flooring with hot water vapor and zero cleansers. They can even be used to clean dirt and grime embedded deep in carpets!

# 163 **Give tile, hardwood, and laminate floors a streak-free shine with a homemade floor cleaner.**

Make your floors spotless, and leave them smelling clean and fresh with this DIY floor cleaner.

1 cup white vinegar

1 tablespoon dish soap

1 cup baking soda

2 gallons warm water

10–15 drops essential oil for scent, if desired (pine is commonly used)

5-gallon bucket

1. Mix the ingredients well in a 5-gallon bucket. Add 10–15 drops of essential oil for fragrance, if desired.
2. Mop your floor as usual.

# 164 **Remove pet hair in no time with a squeegee.**

Run a squeegee over carpets, rugs, and upholstery to remove pet hair the easy way.

## Chemical-Free Ways to Care for Wood Floors

There are so many natural solutions for cleaning wood floors and keeping them looking newly buffed for longer!

**165** **Use a microfiber floor duster to pick up dirt and dust that the vacuum may miss.** Clean the bulk of the mess with a vacuum or broom, then follow up with a microfiber duster to catch as much dust and hair as possible before mopping.

**166** **Deep clean with vinegar.** Add 1 cup of white vinegar to 1 gallon of warm water. Wet a clean mop in the solution, and wring out the extra water until the mop is damp. Mop in the direction of the floorboards so any streaks left behind won't be as noticeable. Allow to air-dry. Use this method to occasionally deep clean dirt and oil buildup.

**167** **Use tea to make floors shine.** Steep 1 bag of black tea in 2 cups of boiling water, and let it sit until it cools to room temperature. Remove the tea bag, soak a clean cloth in the brewed tea, wring it out, and use it to wipe the floor after mopping. The tannic acid in tea gives wood floors a sparkling shine.

**168** **Hide scratches with melted crayon.** Using a crayon that closely matches the color of your flooring, rub the scratches, then soften with a hair dryer. Let it sit for 1–2 minutes, and buff with a microfiber cloth.

**169 Clean pet urine with baking soda.** Wipe up the mess with cloths or paper towels. Spray with all-purpose cleaner, and wipe again. Sprinkle liberally with baking soda, and let it sit overnight. Wipe up the baking soda, and clean with the all-purpose cleaner again. The stain and odor should be gone. Repeat if any scent lingers.

**170 Use a clothes iron to fix dents.** Did you drop something heavy that caused a dent in your wood floor? Spray some water on the spot, and put a damp cloth over it. Carefully iron the dent in a circular motion. The dent should pop right back up.

**171 Apply toothpaste to remove permanent marker.** Squirt a dab of plain white toothpaste on the stain. Scrub with a damp cloth, then wipe clean.

**172 Use vinegar and olive oil to remove scratches and scuff marks.** Mix 1 tablespoon of white vinegar with 3 tablespoons of olive oil. Rub the mixture into the scratches, and watch them disappear! Don't have olive oil? Any liquid vegetable oil will do.

**173 Remove gum with an ice cube.** Freeze the gum with an ice cube, then very carefully scrape it off the floor with a razor blade.

**174 Get rid of pet hair stuck deep in carpets with a pumice stone.** Run a pumice stone over carpets to collect pet hair hidden deep in the fibers.

**175 Use a rubber glove to remove pet hair.** Put on a rubber glove, and use it to pick up pet hair. The hair fibers will stick to the glove.

**176 Clean microfiber furniture with vodka.** Spray vodka on your microfiber couch to freshen and remove stains. Scrub with a light-colored cloth or sponge. Once the area is dry, use a scrub brush to fluff fibers back in place.

**177 Keep your houseplants fungus-free with hydrogen peroxide.** Add 1 tablespoon of hydrogen peroxide to your water bottle the next time you spray your plants to ward off leaf fungus and keep your plants healthy.

## Unexpected Ways to Clean with Hair Spray

Finding alternative uses for items you already have in the house can help you save time, money, and effort on your cleaning routine. Chances are, if you use hair styling products, you already have a can of natural hair spray in your bathroom. Here are some surprising ways to clean with natural hair spray:

178 **Prevent dust buildup on curtains.** Lightly spray window curtains with hair spray to repel dirt and dust.

179 **Remove lint and pet hair from clothes, furniture, and carpets.** Spray hair spray on a clean towel, and use it to remove lint and pet hair.

180 **Kill bug and insect home invaders.** Spray directly on bugs and insects like houseflies, spiders, ants, and more to kill them instantly and stop them from infesting your home.

181 **Remove sticky labels with ease.** Hair spray helps dissolve the adhesive on labels and stickers. Spray the label liberally with hair spray. Let it sit for about 5 minutes, and wipe clean.

182 **Preserve the shine on shoes after polishing.** Give leather shoes a light spray with hair spray after polishing to help the shine last longer.

**183** **Use mayonnaise to make artificial plants shine.**
Faux plants are a wonderful, low-maintenance way to brighten up a room, but dust can make them appear dull and dingy. Put a dab of mayo on a cloth, and wipe leaves to make them shine like new again.

**184** **Make a natural air freshener with vodka and essential oils.** Commercial air fresheners contain toxic fragrances that can act as hormone disrupters, cause asthma in healthy individuals, and maybe even cause cancer! To make your own natural, safe, and effective room spray, mix 1 cup of water, ½ cup of vodka, and 10–15 drops of your favorite essential oil(s) in a spray bottle, and shake to combine. Spray to freshen air and fabrics in your home without the health risks! (This spray works great on smelly shoes too.)

**185** **Use salt to clean faux flowers.** Put the flowers in a 1-gallon plastic storage bag, and add ¾ cup of salt. Shake the bag, and watch the salt get all brown and dingy!

**186** **Remove dirt and smudges from photos and paintings with a slice of bread.** Gently rub a slice of bread on photos and paintings to wipe away dirt and smudges without harming the pictures.

**187** **Clean vent covers effortlessly in the dishwasher.** The little slats in vent covers can be really difficult to get clean. Pop them in the dishwasher, and let it do all the work for you. First, rinse the vent cover in a sink or bucket of soapy water, using a bottle brush to remove as much dirt and debris as possible. Put the vent cover in the dishwasher, and wash on the short cycle with water and no detergent. Let the cover air-dry before placing back on the vent.

**188** **Dust air vents with a cloth and a butter knife.** Wrap a damp cleaning cloth around a butter knife to clean between the thin slats in your air vents. For tough dirt, spray the vent with all-purpose cleaner first, then wipe clean.

# 189

**Assemble your own DIY plug-in refill.** Those plug-in air fresheners contain toxic ingredients too. Make your own homemade plug-in refill with this easy recipe to keep your family safe. Use a pair of pliers to gently pull the wick away from the plug-in container. Rinse the container thoroughly to remove the old chemical fragrance. Fill the container $\frac{1}{3}$ to $\frac{1}{2}$ full with your favorite essential oil, then fill the rest of the way with water. Replace the wick, and push firmly until you hear it click into place. Shake well, and plug into an outlet to distribute the clean, natural fragrance.

- Relax with a blend of lavender and vanilla. Use this scent combination for bedrooms and nighttime TV watching in the living room or den.
- Energize with citrus oils like lemon, orange, and grapefruit. Try these scents in the kitchen and exercise room.
- Focus with peppermint and rosemary. Try this blend when you need to focus and get things done, such as in a home office.
- Deodorize with cinnamon, clove, and tea tree oils. This essential oil combination purifies the air with strong natural scents and antibacterial cleaning power. Use this fragrance throughout your home to clean offensive pet smells and other odors.

# 190 Pull the vacuum cleaner backward slowly for maximum effectiveness.

Many people don't realize that pushing the vacuum forward just directs it where to go. The vacuum is really only cleaning when you pull it backward. To help your vacuum perform even better, pull it back slowly so that it has more time to catch all the dirt.

# 191 Remove mystery carpet stains with hydrogen peroxide.

Don't know what the stain is, but still want it clean? Mix 1 teaspoon of hydrogen peroxide with a little non-gel, plain white toothpaste or a sprinkle of cream of tartar. Work the paste into the stain with a cloth or sponge, then rinse with clean, cool water. This method even works on stubborn bloodstains!

# 192 Save money on floor cleaner with highly concentrated Sal Suds.

Just 1½ teaspoons of Sal Suds per 1 gallon of water is all you need to make bare floors sparkling clean. This solution is safe and effective on all bare floors, even wood! Dip a clean mop in the mixture, and wring it until damp. Mop the floor, and follow up with a dry cloth or air-dry.

**193** **Clean area rugs with a garden hose.** Wool, cotton, and jute rugs will need to be spot-cleaned like indoor carpets, but rugs made of synthetic fibers like nylon and rayon are a bit more forgiving. Of course, you should follow the manufacturer's care instructions if they're available, and do a spot test on the fabric for colorfastness before cleaning the entire rug. If your synthetic area rug needs some serious cleaning, vacuum it, then take it outside, and spray it with the garden hose! A sloped driveway works best for this because you won't have to lay the rug on the dirty grass. Spray the rug with the hose until it's completely wet. Squirt a couple drops of dish soap or Sal Suds, and use a scrub brush to work the soap into the fibers. Don't scrub too vigorously or you may cause damage. Rinse the rug thoroughly with the hose until the suds are completely gone, then leave it outside to dry.

**194** **Scrub away deep stains with a toothbrush.** Apply a stain remover, such as white vinegar, plain (unflavored) club soda, or vodka, and work it into deep stains with a soft-bristled toothbrush. Blot to lift the stain.

## Effective Ways to Care for Carpets

Use these tricks to nix stains and odors in no time, and breathe new life into your carpets!

**195 Freshen with this natural and affordable homemade carpet powder.** Add 20–30 drops of your favorite essential oil to a 16-ounce box of baking soda. Put the flap down on the box, and shake well. Use immediately, or let the mixture sit for 6–8 hours to allow the essential oil fragrance to absorb into the baking soda. Sprinkle generously on smelly carpets. Let it sit for 20 minutes or overnight for tough odors, then vacuum it up. Store the powder in a cool, dry place, and use it on any surface that needs freshening.

**196 Use vinegar and laundry detergent to clean spilled paint.** Work quickly to clean the paint before it dries. Mix 1 tablespoon of white vinegar, 1 tablespoon of laundry detergent, and 2 cups of water. Sponge the solution onto the stain, and blot to remove.

**197 Remove ink stains with milk and cornstarch.** Mix 2 parts milk with 3 parts cornstarch to form a paste, and apply it to the ink stain. Let it sit for a few hours to dry, then vacuum it up. (Cornstarch also works great on oil and grease stains.)

**198** **Clean pet stains and odors with vinegar and baking soda.** Blot away as much of the mess as you can with paper towels. Mix a 50/50 solution of water and white vinegar, and pour it on the stain. Scrub to work the mixture into the carpet. For really smelly messes, use straight vinegar. Sprinkle baking soda onto the carpet to cover the stain, and scrub to work it into the fibers. Add a little of the vinegar mixture to dampen, and continue to work the paste into the carpet. Let it sit for a day or overnight until the baking soda is dry, then vacuum up.

**199** **Iron carpets to remove stains.** Mix a 50/50 solution of water and white vinegar in a spray bottle. Spray the stain liberally with the mixture, and cover with a terry cloth. Iron the terry cloth, and watch as the stain lifts onto the cloth with ease.

**200** **Nix carpet stains with vodka.** Blot the stain to remove most of the mess, then pour any clear alcohol, such as vodka, rubbing alcohol, or even white wine, onto the stain. Continue blotting until the stain lifts away.

**201** **Remove nail polish from carpets with vodka.** Let the nail polish dry, then chip as much off as you can with a knife. Put some vodka on a cloth, and blot the stain until it dissolves away.

## 202 Make your own safe and natural carpet cleaning solution for machines.

Get your whole carpet clean without dangerous chemicals with this simple and inexpensive DIY carpet cleaner. Please note, when mixing hydrogen peroxide with other ingredients, plan to use the solution right away, and discard any remaining mixture.

3 quarts hot water

¼ cup white vinegar

3 tablespoons natural dish soap

1 cup hydrogen peroxide

¼ teaspoon essential oils (optional)

1. Use the hottest water you can get from the tap and add to a large pot. Add the rest of the ingredients, and stir gently to combine. Add your favorite essential oils for scent, if desired.

2. Pour the solution into your carpet cleaning machine, and follow the manufacturer's directions for use.

# FURNITURE

**203** **Vacuum the tiniest cracks with a squeeze bottle cap.** Take the top off of a squeeze bottle—the inexpensive, reusable ones used for condiments—and put it on the end of your vacuum's attachment hose to clean tiny spaces in furniture and throughout your home that even a crevice tool can't reach.

**204** **Make your own dusting gloves out of old socks.** Now you know what to do with those stray socks from the laundry—turn them into handy dusting gloves! Put a sock on your hand, spray lightly with all-purpose spray, and wipe surfaces clean. Kids love this cleaning method.

**205** **Hide scuffs on wood with walnuts.** Rub a walnut into scuffs and scratches. The color from the walnut will blend into the wood, making small marks less noticeable.

**206** **Remove spilled wax from wood with ice.** Fill a storage bag with ice cubes, and put it on the wax. Let it sit for a few minutes until the wax hardens, then scrape it away easily.

**207** **Eliminate water stains with mayonnaise.** Apply a thick layer of mayo to the stain, and let it sit for 24 hours for light stains and up to 48 hours for tougher jobs. Wipe clean with a cloth.

**208** **Use a hair dryer to fix new water stains.** You can also use a hair dryer to fix water stain emergencies in wood furniture. Blow the hair dryer on the stain until it dries, then seal with a dab of olive oil.

**209** **Freshen fabrics with baking soda.** Sprinkle some baking soda on fabric couches, chairs, and love seats. Let it sit for 30 minutes, then vacuum them clean.

# 210 Renew upholstery with this DIY upholstery cleaner.
Has that upholstered chair or couch seen better days? Make it look bright and new again with this easy and inexpensive DIY upholstery cleaner.

1 cup water or plain (unflavored) club soda

½ cup white vinegar

½ tablespoon natural dish soap

Spray bottle

1. Mix the ingredients in a spray bottle. Vacuum upholstery to lift loose dirt from the surface, and do a spot test with the cleaner before use.
2. If the fabric is easily removable (e.g., a dining room chair with removable seat), remove it before cleaning. Spray the cleaner on upholstery until the surface is lightly soaked, and let it sit for 5–10 minutes. Scrub lightly in a circular motion with a cloth or sponge to lift stains. Do not scrub too hard or the fabric may pill. Spray with water, and mop up extra moisture with a wet/dry vac or a dry, absorbent cloth.
3. Once the upholstery is completely dry, vacuum again to make sure all the dirt is out of the fabric.

**211** **Use a dry homemade cleaner to clean fabrics that shouldn't get wet.** Mix ½ cup of baking soda with ½ cup of cornstarch. Add just enough water to form a thick paste. Apply the paste to fabric, and allow it to dry (this should take about 30 minutes). When the paste is dry, vacuum the fabric clean. If you want a completely dry cleaner, sprinkle the baking soda and cornstarch on the fabric, and vacuum it clean. It may not have as much cleaning power as the paste, but baking soda and cornstarch will still draw out dirt and neutralize odors.

**212** **Spot-treat tough stains with DIY upholstery stain remover.** Mix 1 cup of rubbing alcohol with 1 cup of white vinegar in a spray bottle. Spray the stain, and let it sit for 1–2 minutes. Scrub the stain with a clean towel or sponge, then let it dry. Repeat if needed. Warning: do not use alcohol on fabrics containing acrylic, modacrylic, acetate, or triacetate fibers.

**213** **Hide small scratches in leather with shoe polish.** Use shoe polish that most closely matches the color of the leather. Apply a little shoe polish on scratches, and buff dry.

**214 Clean leather furniture with a homemade citrus spray.** Place 1 cup of white vinegar, 2 tablespoons of olive oil, 6 tablespoons of coconut oil, and 8–10 drops of orange or lemon essential oil in a spray bottle. Screw on the lid and shake well to combine. Do a spot test with the cleaning spray on a hidden area before treating the entire piece, and wait 24–48 hours to ensure the spray won't cause any damage to the leather. If the leather looks great after the spot test, spray the cleaner on a cloth, and wipe the leather clean. Let it sit for 20 minutes, then wipe again with a dry cloth.

**215 Make wood shine with beer.** Spot-check in an inconspicuous place before wiping down the entire piece. Wet a cloth with flat beer, and wring it out until damp and not soaking. Wipe dull wood in circular motions to make it look shiny and new again. Follow up with a dry cloth to remove any excess moisture left behind. The B vitamins and sugar content in beer add luster to wood surfaces.

**216 Condition leather with olive oil.** Use an old washcloth or paper towels to apply olive oil to scratched and dried-out leather on couches, love seats, and other furniture. Add more oil to particularly dry spots, and let it sit for 5–10 minutes to absorb. Wipe thoroughly with a clean, dry (old) towel to remove excess oil.

## Surefire Ways to Polish Brass Furniture and Fixtures

Brass is a material commonly used in furniture and household fixtures, but it can get dull and tarnished over the years. Here are some quick and easy ways to clean solid and brass-plated items to make them look shiny and new again!

**217** **Use a magnet to see if your item is solid or plated brass.** It's important to know whether your brass object is solid brass or plated brass because the cleaning methods are different. Use a refrigerator magnet to find out. If the magnet sticks, it's plated brass, and if it doesn't, you have a solid piece.

**218** **Employ gentle methods to clean brass-plated items.** If the item is plated brass, you'll need to be careful not to scratch the surface and remove the plating, so don't use harsh cleaning methods. Just wipe clean with a cloth dipped in warm, soapy water, and dry thoroughly.

**219** **Clean lightly soiled brass with water and dish soap.** Wipe solid brass with a damp microfiber cloth. If that doesn't get it clean, dip the cloth in some soapy water, or completely submerge smaller pieces in a sink of water and natural dish soap. Use a soft toothbrush to clean inside cracks and crevices. Rinse and dry thoroughly.

**220 Remove tougher stains and tarnish with ketchup.** The acid in tomatoes does an amazing job at cleaning brass. To clean with ketchup, apply it with a cloth, wipe dirt away, and rinse thoroughly. You can also use tomato juice if you don't have ketchup on hand.

**221 Make brass clean and shiny with lemon juice.** Acidic lemon juice also does a great job on brass. For light tarnish, cut a lemon in half, sprinkle some cooking salt on the cut side, and use that to scrub the tarnish away. Wipe away the salt and lemon juice with a damp cloth, and buff with a dry cloth to make it shine.

**222 Whip up a cleaning paste with salt, vinegar, and flour.** Mix 1 teaspoon of salt with ½ cup of white vinegar. Add enough flour to form a thick paste, and apply the paste to the brass. Let it sit for about 10 minutes, rinse with warm water, and buff dry.

**223 Use lemon and cream of tartar on heavy tarnish.** For tougher jobs, make a paste with 2 parts cream of tartar and 1 part lemon juice. Apply the paste, and let it sit for 30 minutes to an hour. Rinse with warm water, dry thoroughly, and buff with a clean, dry cloth. Cream of tartar is not only mildly abrasive—it also acts as a natural bleach to quickly lift stains away.

**224** **Make your own brass polish with water, vinegar, and salt.** Mix 2 cups of hot water with 1 tablespoon each of white vinegar and salt, and stir gently until the salt dissolves. Dip a cloth in the solution, and use it to polish brass after cleaning. Wipe dry with a clean cloth.

**225** **Keep brass clean with linseed oil.** Now that you've cleaned your solid or brass-plated items, protect them with a coat of linseed oil. While linseed oil is the best option, you can also use other natural cooking oils if that's all you have on hand.

**226** **Be careful cleaning antiques yourself.** You may want to take your tarnished brass antique to an appraiser and have them professionally cleaned instead of doing it yourself. Some antiques are actually worth more tarnished, or the object may lose value if you damage it trying to clean it yourself.

227 **Never spray cleaning sprays directly on electronics.** Moisture and electrical devices are a bad combination. To prevent damage, never spray an electronic device with any liquid, including cleaning sprays. When using a spray cleaner, spray the cleaning cloth, then use it to wipe the device.

228 **Dust electronics with coffee filters.** Static cling can make dusting electronics difficult even with microfiber cloths. Wipe dust and pet hair away with a dry coffee filter, then follow up with a damp microfiber cloth, if desired, to keep dirt and dust away longer.

229 **Clean and sanitize your remote with vodka.** To kill germs on your remote, spray a cloth with vodka or hydrogen peroxide, and wipe clean. Clean between the buttons with a cotton swab.

## 230 Use a damp microfiber cloth to clean screens.

Television, computer, and LCD screens are all very delicate, so it's best to keep things simple when cleaning. If your screen is just dusty, use a dry microfiber cloth to wipe it clean. To clean streaks and spots, wet the microfiber cloth with warm water, and wring out as much water as you can. Wipe gently, being careful not to put any pressure on the screen, then buff with a polishing cloth for a streak-free shine.

## 231 Remove oils from your keyboard with vodka.

Turn off your keyboard if it's wireless, or unplug it if it's wired. Remove dust and food crumbs from between the keys by lightly shaking the keyboard over a trash can, then wipe the entire keyboard with a microfiber cloth sprayed lightly with vodka or white vinegar to remove oils, fingerprints, and light sticky food messes.

## 232 Brush dirt away from your keyboard with a toothbrush.

Use a slightly dampened toothbrush to clean down deep, where cleaning cloths can't reach.

**233** **Clean really grimy keyboard messes with a cotton swab.** To remove caked-on or very old dirt from your keyboard, dip a cotton swab in vodka or white vinegar. Use the cotton swab to scrub away tough dirt, then wipe clean with a microfiber cloth or paper towel.

**234** **Suck up dust and crumbs with your vacuum cleaner.** If your keyboard is really messy, clean it with your vacuum's crevice tool or with a handheld vacuum.

**235** **Remove dirt and debris from the tiniest cracks using toothpicks.** With their tiny, pointed ends, toothpicks can clean in very hard-to-reach areas! Remove lint, dirt, and debris from USB ports in smartphones and computers, cracks and crevices in cameras, and more, by scraping gently with a toothpick, then wiping clean.

**236** **Use cotton swabs to clean and disinfect earbuds.** Put a tiny bit of vodka on a cotton swab, and use it to gently wipe away dirt and germs from your earbuds.

**237** **Clean touchscreens with water.** Manufacturers recommend cleaning touchscreens with water only. These devices, which include smartphones and touchscreen computers, have a coating on them that reduces fingerprints and smudges. Using white vinegar, vodka, or other ingredients commonly used in natural cleaning can harm or even remove this protective coating.
To clean these devices, wet a microfiber cloth with warm water, and wring out as much water as you can to make a slightly damp cleaning cloth. Wipe the device to remove dust, fingerprints, and oils, then buff dry with a polishing cloth.

**238** **Dust speakers with a lint roller.** Run a lint roller over computer and stereo speakers to clean dust and hair away easily.

**239** **Clean a dirty fitness tracker band with vodka.** Wipe your fitness tracker band with a cloth dipped in vodka to remove sweat and germs without leaving residue that may irritate skin.

# 4. BEDROOMS

We spend about ⅓ of our lives in bed. Since sleep deprivation can have a huge impact on your quality of life and even your life expectancy, it's important to make sure your bedroom is a clean, tidy, and relaxing space.

# Your Bedroom Deep-Cleaning Checklist

Get your bedroom cleaner than ever before—and keep it that way—with these easy step-by-step tips.

**240** **Pick up clothes and clutter.** Better yet, try to make it a habit to keep your room tidy all the time. Toss dirty clothes straight in the clothes hamper after wearing. If your dirty laundry never makes it to the chair or floor, it doesn't just look better—it's also one fewer step you need to clean the room. Also, give everything a place. Get a bookshelf for your books and a shoe rack for your shoes.

**241** **Strip the bed.** Wash your sheets every week, pillow covers every month, mattress covers every 3 months, and your comforter and pillows every 6 months or when soiled.

**242** **Rotate your mattress.** Rotate the position of your mattress every 3 months to keep it from sagging. This is especially important when you share a bed with a partner because this can quickly cause uneven wear on your mattress.

**243** **Clean and tidy the closet.** Tidy clothes, shoes, and other stored items. Wipe down the walls and doors with a damp microfiber cloth, if needed. Vacuum the floor.

**244** **Dust all surfaces.** Work from top to bottom so you won't have to clean anything twice. Dust the ceiling fan with a pillowcase. Dust the furniture with a damp microfiber cloth. Don't forget the baseboards, light fixtures, and switches. If needed, wash the walls with a microfiber mop.

**245** **Wipe windows and mirrors.** Get a streak-free shine with microfiber and polishing cloths. Wipe with a damp microfiber cloth, then buff with a dry polishing cloth.

**246** **Clean the floors.** Vacuum carpets, or sweep, vacuum, and mop hardwood floors. Launder throw rugs at least once a month or when soiled. Clean under the bed with vacuum attachments.

**247** **Vacuum the drapes.** Clean the drapes with your vacuum's upholstery attachment. If they're machine washable, toss them in the washer every 1–2 months.

**248** **Make the bed neatly.** Take your sheets straight from the dryer to your bed to prevent wrinkles from folding. Plus, who doesn't love crawling into a nice, warm, freshly made bed?! Enjoy your wonderfully clean room!

# LINENS

**249** **Make your bed every day to improve sleep quality and keep your bedroom tidy.** That's right—making your bed may seem like just another annoying and unnecessary chore, but a National Sleep Foundation poll found that most people say making their bed every morning improves their sleep quality. Making your bed every morning also keeps your sheets clean, your bedroom neat and tidy, and your bed linens newer longer, and it may help you start your day off right.

**250** **Hang shirts so that they'll stay put.** Hang the shirt as usual, and thread the clothing tag at the neck of the shirt through the hook of the clothes hanger to prevent the garment from sliding off the hanger.

**251** **Save time finding linen sets in your linen closet by storing sheet sets in pillowcases.** Store each set of sheets together in a pillowcase to keep your linen closet neat and organized. When you make your bed, you can just grab a set and go.

## 252 Get a better night's rest with DIY lavender linen spray.

Lavender essential oil has a calming effect on the body and helps reduce stress and improve sleep quality. This homemade spray will freshen linens between washes, so you can sleep better and wake up feeling rejuvenated! Never use essential oils around cats and birds. Lavender is considered safe for use around children and dogs.

2 tablespoons witch hazel or vodka

10 drops lavender essential oil

6 tablespoons water

4-ounce glass spray bottle

1. Add the witch hazel or vodka and lavender essential oil to the spray bottle.
2. Cover the bottle opening with your finger, and shake well to combine. (Essential oils don't emulsify with water, and this step will help all the ingredients mix together.)
3. Add the water, screw on the spray cap, and shake again to combine. Use this spray on your pillows and linens anytime they need refreshing.

# 253 Wash your bedsheets at least once a week.

Sweat causes bacteria to grow on your sheets, and skin cells attract dust mites and bedbugs, which can aggravate allergies, asthma, and other health issues. If you are sick or you perspire a lot, wash more often than once a week. Wash and dry your sheets on the hottest settings allowed for the fabric.

# 254 Use all your space by storing belongings under the bed.

Some beds have built-in storage. You can use the same idea even if you don't have this type of bed by storing items in flat plastic bins or repurposed old dresser drawers. To make dresser drawers easy to move, install 4 little wheels on the bottoms of the drawers so they can be wheeled in and out easily.

# 255 Store bulky clothes and linens in vacuum storage bags.

You can store bulky comforters, sweaters, blankets, coats, and more without taking up so much space if you suck the air out of the bags. Put your bulky items in the special bags and seal them. Vacuum out the air to make it nice and compact.

# MATTRESSES AND PILLOWS

**256** **Vacuum your mattress when you rotate it.** You should rotate your mattress every 3 months to prevent sagging. Since you'll be moving it around anyway, you can use the upholstery attachment from your vacuum to remove dirt and allergens from in between the mattress and box spring and under the bed.

**257** **Use waterproof protective covers to protect against pet and kid stains.** Think of this as an insurance policy to help your investments stay like new.

**258** **Improve and prevent allergy problems with hypoallergenic bedding.** Allergens, bedbugs, dust mites, and molds can all take up residence in your mattress, making you susceptible to a host of health problems. Hypoallergenic bedding includes mattress and box spring covers, pillow covers, comforters, blankets, and sheets. Signs that you may need to use hypoallergenic bedding include allergy symptoms, such as coughing, sneezing, runny nose, wheezing, difficulty breathing, congestion, and watery eyes; bedbugs on your mattress or bites on your body; and damp and musty bedding.

# Easy Ways to Make Your Mattress Last

Mattresses typically last about 5–10 years before they need to be replaced. You can protect your investment and try to stretch that time a little further with these tips.

**259 Let fresh air in.** Be sure to open those light-blocking window treatments once in a while. When you wash your linens, open your windows, and let sunlight and fresh air come in. Doing this will air out the mattress and chase dust mites and bedbugs away.

**260 Use a mattress cover.** Mattresses aren't cheap. To protect your investment, use a mattress cover to keep dead skin cells, sweat, pet stains, dust mites, and more from penetrating your mattress. Plus, mattress covers are much easier to clean than a big, absorbent mattress, so they help allergies and asthma problems immensely.

**261 Don't jump on the bed.** Jumping on the bed may be fun, but it can cause damage to your mattress that can reduce its support and shorten its life span.

**262 Store it correctly.** If you need to store your mattress, cover it with a breathable cover made for storage, and store it flat in a climate-controlled storage unit. Also, be sure not to lay any heavy objects on top of your mattress. Basements are too damp for mattress storage, and garages are prone to humidity and temperature changes that may harm your mattress with prolonged exposure.

**263** **Wash your bed linens often enough.** Wash your sheets every week to clean pet hair and dander, sweat, bacteria, and other yucky messes that, if left unchecked, can penetrate into your mattress.

**264** **Be sure to support your mattress properly.** Traditional mattresses need box springs, while the newer foam mattresses work best on foundations. Follow the manufacturer's directions for the support of your mattress since incorrect support can make the bed uncomfortable for you and shorten the life span of the mattress.

**265** **Rotate your mattress.** You should rotate your mattress from top to bottom about every 3 months to avoid sagging spots and other issues.

**266** **Clean the mattress.** Vacuum your mattress at least every 3 months when you rotate it to control dust mites and other allergens.

**267** **Don't allow your dog to sleep under the bed.** Letting your dog sleep under the bed may seem harmless enough, but the hair and dander left behind can aggravate allergies and asthma, and your pup can accidentally tear the lining of your mattress or box spring. Give your dog his own bed to sleep on instead.

# 268 Freshen your mattress with a DIY mattress cleaner.

This easy DIY mattress cleaner freshens, deodorizes, and repels dust mites, which is one of the biggest causes of indoor allergies. Essential oils should not be used around cats and birds. Children and dogs may also be sensitive to some of the oils in this recipe. Consult your pediatrician and/or veterinarian before using this essential oil mixture in your home.

1 cup baking soda

10 drops essential oil (lavender, clove, eucalyptus, peppermint, rosemary, basil, and lemongrass all naturally repel bugs, including dust mites and bedbugs)

1 Combine the ingredients in a bowl, then use a baking sifter to dust the mixture evenly over your mattress.

2 Let it sit for an hour before vacuuming it clean. Use this mattress cleaner every time you clean your mattress pad.

**269** **Disinfect with vodka.** Mattresses can harbor loads of bacteria in the form of sweat, pet dander, dust mites, and more. You don't have to stop sharing your bed with your favorite pooch; just clean it up! Fill a spray bottle with vodka or hydrogen peroxide, and add 10–15 drops of your favorite essential oil. Lavender is a great essential oil to use in the bedroom since it has a calming effect, can help you sleep, and is safe for use around children and dogs. (Please note that lavender essential oil is not safe for use around cats and birds.) Shake to combine, then spray your mattress liberally. Allow to air-dry before making your bed. This trick also works great on pillows and bedding between washes.

**270** **Use vinegar and baking soda to clean and deodorize vomit stains.** Mix ½ cup each of white vinegar and water in a spray bottle. Spray the stain, and blot with a clean cloth. Repeat these steps until the stain is gone, then sprinkle the area with baking soda to deodorize. Let it sit for 1–2 hours, and vacuum it clean. Make sure the mattress is completely dry before you make the bed.

**271** **Zap bloodstains on your mattress with a homemade hydrogen peroxide paste.** Be sure to use a white cloth to wipe or blot—colored cloths may stain the mattress. Please note, when mixing hydrogen peroxide with other ingredients, plan to use the solution right away, and discard any remaining mixture.

1 tablespoon liquid dish soap

1 tablespoon salt

¼ cup hydrogen peroxide

1 Mix the ingredients together, then apply the thick paste to the stain.

2 Let it sit until completely dry, then wipe away the residue with a damp cloth. If the stain isn't completely gone, take a white rag, and blot with hydrogen peroxide until the stain lifts away.

**272** **Clean and freshen pet beds in a snap with baking soda.** Sprinkle your pet's bed liberally with baking soda. Let it sit for at least 30 minutes, then vacuum it clean. Warning: be careful using essential oils to clean pet beds and supplies, since some pets may be sensitive to certain oils. Never use essential oils around cats and birds.

# 273 Remove urine and sweat stains with a homemade disinfecting spray.

For soaking urine stains, first absorb as much liquid as you can with paper towels. Please note, when mixing hydrogen peroxide with other ingredients, plan to use the solution right away, and discard any remaining mixture.

1 cup hydrogen peroxide

3 tablespoons baking soda

1 teaspoon natural dish soap

Spray bottle

1. Stir the ingredients together gently in a bowl until the baking soda dissolves.
2. Put the mixture in a spray bottle, and spray the stain liberally.
3. Let it sit for at least 1–2 hours to dry. Direct a fan toward the mattress to speed up the drying process. Prevent future stains with a waterproof mattress cover.

# DUST MITES AND BEDBUGS

Dust mites and their droppings are one of the leading causes of year-round allergies and asthma. If you wake up with red, itchy bumps on your body, you may be suffering from dust mite allergies. Other symptoms include sneezing; coughing; stuffy or runny nose; red or watery eyes; and itching of the skin, eyes, nose, mouth, or throat. Here are some simple and effective natural cleaning tips that will help you get dust mites out of your home for good.

## 274 Protect yourself when you clean.
Allergy sufferers benefit from living in a clean home, but cleaning can also make allergies worse, as dust and other allergens become airborne as you clean. If you're allergic to dust mites, pollen, dander, or other allergens, wear a filtering face mask when cleaning to reduce exposure.

## 275 Don't make your bed.
Finally, an excuse to be lazy! Dust mites love humidity. Airing out your mattress and bed covers will allow humidity to evaporate from your bed, making the area less favorable for dust mites and bacteria growth. After you get up in the morning, pull the covers back to let heat and humidity escape. You can always come back and make your bed later if you like.

**276 Wash bedsheets in hot water.** Dust mites can't survive temperatures higher than 130°F to 140°F. Wash sheets and blankets once a week and other soft furnishings, such as rugs, cushions, and throws, once or twice a month.

**277 Control heat and humidity.** Dust mites thrive in warm, humid conditions. If you live in a humid area, use a dehumidifier to keep humidity levels in your home below 50% (the ideal humidity in your home is between 30% and 40%). Keep room temperatures between 65°F and 72°F, especially in the bedroom where dust mite populations are highest. Bonus: cooler temperatures also help you sleep better!

**278 Make your own dust mite spray.** Dust mites hate the smell of certain essential oils, including eucalyptus, clove, lavender, peppermint, rosemary, basil, and lemongrass. Make your own repellent spray by filling a spray bottle with water and adding a few drops of one or more of these essential oils. A mixture of basil and lemongrass oils is a great combination for repelling dust mites, fleas, and lice. Spray your bed, and let it air-dry. Be careful using essential oils around children and dogs, since they may be sensitive to certain oils. Never use essential oils around cats and birds.

**279 Dust with a damp cloth.** Dusting with a dry cloth won't get rid of dust mites. In fact, dry dusting can actually cause them to become airborne and aggravate allergies even more. Dampen a clean cloth with water or DIY cleaning spray to stop dust mites in their tracks.

**280 Cover your mattress and pillows.** Keep dust mites and other pests and allergens off your sleeping surfaces with mite-proof covers. Simply launder covers, as needed, to keep your bed fresh and clean.

**281 Put your pillows in the freezer to kill pests.** Washing your pillows can cause them to break down before their time. To kill pests without washing, put your pillows in a plastic garbage bag, and throw them in the freezer for a few hours every month.

**282 Vacuum often.** Vacuum rugs, mattresses, pillows, drapes, upholstery, and other soft items in your home at least once a week using your vacuum's upholstery attachment. Use a vacuum cleaner with a HEPA filter to trap airborne dust particles.

**283 Lose the clutter.** Clutter collects dust—and, therefore, dust mites! To clean up your space, try to adopt a more minimalistic approach to decorating. Reduce the number of unnecessary objects like knick-knacks, stacks of paper, magazines, and books in your home. Clearing clutter will not only help you fight dust and dust mites; it will also make it easier to clean your home and may even reduce your stress levels!

**284 Introduce air-purifying houseplants.** House-plants can have many benefits, including purifying the air, giving your home a pop of vibrant color, and even helping you get more restful sleep at night. Just like other surfaces in your home, your houseplants can accumulate dust and provide a cozy home for dust mites, so make sure you dust their leaves to keep pests and allergens at bay.

**285 Clean air vents.** Dust and dust mites can build up in your air ducts, causing dirt, dust, and allergens to continually circulate throughout your home. Keep vents clean by regularly vacuuming and wiping them down with a damp cloth. Use high-performance filters designed for allergen reduction, and change them regularly to keep household air clean.

**286** **Change your flooring.** Homes with bare floors have up to 90% less dust than carpeted homes! Choose wooden floors or tiles instead of carpeting, and decorate with rugs that can be washed regularly.

**287** **Clean up after pets.** Pets with fur or feathers release dander, which is a prime food source for dust mites. Groom pets outdoors, if possible, and keep them off human bedding and couches. Regularly wash pet beds and blankets in high heat, and cover pet beds with allergen-proof covers. Pets can also suffer from dust mite allergies, so it's important to keep their living spaces clean too.

**288** **Sprinkle diatomaceous earth.** Apply food-grade diatomaceous earth (DE) powder to the affected area. Let the powder sit for a few hours, and vacuum it up along with all the dead dust mites and other bugs and insects it came in contact with.

## A Simple System to Eliminate Bedbugs Naturally

Once your bedroom is infested, bedbugs are difficult to get rid of, but luckily, natural remedies are just as effective as commercial chemical treatments *and* are much safer and more cost-effective. How do you know you have bedbugs? Check for them around your mattress and furniture. Since they're much bigger than dust mites, you can see them with the naked eye if you look closely, and they leave behind telltale blood smears and black fecal matter on your linens and mattress. Bedbugs also feed on you while you sleep, so you'll probably suffer from bites and rashes.

289 **Get out the steam cleaner.** Just like dust mites, bedbugs can't live in high temperatures above 130°F. Steam clean your linens, mattress, furniture, curtains, floors, and other soft surfaces. You can buy steam cleaners in stores and online, or rent a commercial unit from a professional exterminator.

290 **Launder all washable fabrics.** Strip your bed. Wash and dry all your bedding in hot water, then store in sealable plastic bags or bins until your bedroom is completely treated.

**291 Vacuum everything.** Thorough vacuuming is very effective against bedbug infestations. Use your vacuum's crevice tool to get in tight spots. Vacuum your mattress and between your mattress and box spring. Put a total encasement mattress cover on your bed to protect your mattress. If you have a carpet cleaner, use it to deep clean the carpets. Once you're done vacuuming, immediately empty the bagless canister or throw away the bag, and take the garbage outside to keep the bugs from escaping back into your home.

**292 Sprinkle diatomaceous earth.** Wear a face mask to prevent breathing in the dust, and sprinkle food-grade diatomaceous earth all over your mattress and box spring and around the legs of your bed. Sprinkle it onto flooring, and work it into carpets. Let it sit for as long as you can—a couple of weeks is great! Then vacuum thoroughly to remove the powder and dead bedbugs. Use a wet/dry vac to clean up diatomaceous earth if possible since it can harm regular household vacuums and even burn up the motor with repeated use.

**293 Repeat.** Since bedbugs are so difficult to get rid of, you'll probably have to repeat these steps at least a few times until the infestation is completely gone. Be vigilant. If you're consistent, you will win.

294 **Polish silver jewelry with mayonnaise.** Apply a liberal dab of mayo on jewelry, and rub with a cloth to remove dirt and tarnish. Wipe away mayo, then polish to a shine with a dry, white cloth. Toothpaste works great too!

295 **Use plain white toothpaste to make rings sparkle.** Put plain nongritty toothpaste on a soft bristled toothbrush, and add a little water as if you were brushing your teeth. Gently scrub your ring in a circular motion, rinse well, and dry with a soft cloth.

296 **Protect costume jewelry with clear nail polish.** Paint your costume jewelry with a clear coat of nail polish to keep pieces from tarnishing and protect your skin from allergic reactions. You can also use nail polish to repair loose stones. or fix faux pearl jewelry and buttons.

# OTHER BEDROOM ITEMS

**297** **Use cornstarch to remove dirt and grease from stuffed animals.** Put stuffed animals in a garbage bag, sprinkle liberally with cornstarch, and shake vigorously. Vacuum or shake outdoors to remove the cornstarch.

**298** **Remove furniture dents from your carpet with ice cubes.** Do you like to move your bedroom furniture but hate the carpet dents they leave behind? Place ice cubes in the dents, and let them melt. Vacuum the wet areas to fluff up the carpet fibers.

**299** **Clean mold and mildew from your humidifier with hydrogen peroxide.** Deep clean your humidifier at least monthly to ensure you and your home stay healthy and clean. Wash your humidifier with soap and water. Rinse well, then spray liberally with hydrogen peroxide to disinfect and remove mold and mildew. Let it sit for 5 minutes, then rinse again. Disinfect inside the unit by adding 2 cups of hydrogen peroxide per 1 gallon of water, then run the machine normally.

**300** **Keep your drawers and closets smelling fresh with candles.** Store natural candles in closed spaces like drawers and closets to keep your clothes and linens smelling sweet.

**301** **Silence squeaky bureau drawers with an old candle.** Rub beeswax or an old candle where the wood is hitting to make the squeaky noise. Push the drawer in and out a few times to distribute the wax. Reapply when the drawer starts squeaking again.

**302** **Use a humidifier to moisten the air, protect your home, and help you sleep.** The ideal humidity in your home is between 30% and 40%, but air tends to dry out in cooler months to as low as 15%! This dry air can cause a number of issues, including home and furniture damage; dry skin, nose, throat, and lips; and health problems that can disrupt your sleep. To moisten the air and help keep you healthy all winter long, use a cool-mist humidifier in your bedroom and in other rooms in your house, such as the living room and den.

**3O3** **Purify the air with essential oils.** Essential oils have many therapeutic benefits for you and your home, including removing dust and bacteria from the air, opening airways, improving mood, and aiding sleep quality. Using a nebulizing essential oil diffuser in your bedroom is an excellent way to clean the air and enjoy the health benefits of essential oils while you sleep. The best scents for improving air and sleep quality include lavender, chamomile, cedarwood, bergamot, sandalwood, and ylang-ylang. You can also enjoy the relaxing benefits of lavender by placing some fresh or dried flowers on your nightstand. Be careful using essential oils around children and dogs, since they may be sensitive to certain oils. Never use essential oils around cats and birds.

**3O4** **Use an air purifier to remove even more dust and allergens.** If anyone in your household suffers from allergies, talk to your doctor about whether you should keep an air purifier in the bedroom to remove dust, pollen, pet dander, and other allergens that can trigger allergies, sinus, and asthma problems that may also keep you up at night. You can use a Himalayan salt lamp as a natural air purifier, or if you prefer an electronic device, try a HEPA air purifier or an ionizing air purifier

# 5. BATHROOMS

Bathrooms have a host of cleaning issues: soap scum, hair spray, moisture, hard water, limescale, and more. Learn how to clean the toughest messes—even rust, mold, and mildew—without dangerous chemicals!

# SCOURING AND POLISHING

**305** **Make a difficult-to-clean showerhead sparkle with almost no effort.** Fill a plastic food bag with white vinegar and a few drops of lemon essential oil, and secure the bag on your showerhead with a rubber band or elastic hair tie. The next morning, remove the bag, and wipe your showerhead clean. This method also works great on faucets.

**306** **Work from the cleanest area to the dirtiest to save on cleaning rags.** Organize your bathroom cleaning schedule so that you start cleaning the "cleanest" area and end with the "dirtiest" (i.e., the toilet). If you clean your toilet first, you'll need to use a new paper towel or cloth to clean your tub or sink, but if you start with the cleanest area, you may be able to use just one cloth.

**307** **Buff chrome with toothpaste.** Put a dab of plain white toothpaste on a cloth, and use it to make chrome fixtures clean and shiny.

**308** **Wash your plastic shower curtain liner with your bath towels.** Pop your shower curtain liner in the washer, and let the machine do all the work. Add your laundry soap and 1 cup of baking soda, then add a few towels to help scrub away soap scum and mildew and keep the curtain from ripping. Once the wash cycle ends, immediately remove the liner and hang it back up in the shower to dry.

**309** **Deep clean your exhaust fan by taking it apart.** Sometimes your exhaust fan will get so greasy and grimy that you'll need to take it apart and give it a deep cleaning. Gently pull the fan cover to remove it from the base. If the cover is really filthy, drop it in a bucket filled with hot water and dish soap, and let it soak while you clean the rest of the fan. Unplug the fan to prevent electric shock, then remove any screws holding the fan and motor in place. Carefully remove the fan and the motor. Wipe clean with a cloth repeatedly dipped in soapy water to remove stuck-on dirt and grease. Use your vacuum's crevice tool to remove dust and debris from the fan base still attached to the ceiling, then wipe it clean with a damp cloth. Once all the other components are clean, scrub the fan cover with a brush or sponge, then rinse thoroughly. Dry everything completely before putting the fan back together.

**310** **Use plain white toothpaste to clean grout stains.** Apply toothpaste on a toothbrush. Use it to scrub grout stains away easily, then rinse.

**311** **Keep cleaning sprays organized with a tension rod.** Store your bathroom cleaning supplies in the cabinet beneath the bathroom sink for easy access. Install a tension rod in the cabinet, and hang spray bottles on it to organize multiple spray bottles and save room on storage.

**312** **Use a shoe organizer for extra product storage.** Install an over-the-door shoe organizer on your bathroom door or in your linen closet to reduce clutter in your bathroom cabinets.

# 313 Make all-natural bathroom cleaning spray

**in no time.** With soap scum, limescale, hair spray, and more, your bathroom can be a tough room to clean. Use this bathroom cleaning spray to cut through even the toughest dirt and grime and kill bacteria to make the job so much easier!

¾ cup baking soda

3 tablespoons salt

½ cup white vinegar

3 tablespoons dish liquid (without Castile soap)

Essential oil for scent, if desired (citrus and eucalyptus oils kill germs and clean soap scum)

Spray bottle

1 Pour all the ingredients in a spray bottle, and add a few drops of your favorite essential oil(s) for fragrance, if desired.

2 Shake before each use, spray surfaces, and wipe clean.

314 **Wash your toothbrush holder in the dish-washer.** Toothbrush holders can get seriously grimy if they're not cleaned regularly. Instead of struggling to scrub it clean, let the dishwasher do all the work. Pop it in the top rack of the dishwasher to clean it effortlessly. This trick also works great for other bathroom accessories, including cups and soap dishes.

315 **Make your own scouring paste with baking soda.** Scour sinks, showers, and tubs with 1 cup of baking soda mixed with water or liquid soap to form a thick paste. Scrub as usual, and rinse clean.

316 **Nix water spots with lemon.** Rub a cut fresh lemon on chrome fixtures to remove water spots. Let it sit for a few minutes, and rinse with water and a microfiber cloth. This method can be used anywhere in your home, but it is especially great at removing mineral deposits and soap scum in the bathroom. Just be sure to test surfaces before applying since lemon can fade certain colors.

**317** **Wax chrome fixtures to make them shine.** Use waxed paper to polish chrome and prevent water spots. Clean and dry your fixtures, then rub the waxy side on the chrome. This trick can also be used on the shower curtain rod to help the shower curtain glide across more easily.

**318** **Use shaving cream to polish chrome.** Shaving cream also works great on chrome fixtures to give them a streak-free shine. Apply a dab of shaving cream to chrome, and buff with a damp cloth.

**319** **Save money by making your own bathroom foaming hand soap refills.** Keep that empty foaming soap dispenser, and refill it with water and 1–2 teaspoons of liquid Castile soap or natural dish soap. Add 15–20 drops of your favorite essential oil for an aromatherapy boost. Ylang-ylang, patchouli, and lavender are all great choices for bathrooms.

# 320 Kill germs with all-natural DIY disinfecting wipes. Keep these wipes on your counter to quickly clean and disinfect bathroom surfaces.

1½ cups water

½ cup vodka

3 tablespoons liquid Castile soap or Sal Suds

40–50 drops grapefruit essential oil

Washcloths or other soft fabric squares

1-quart glass Mason jar (widemouthed jars work best for easy access)

1. Mix the ingredients in a Mason jar or other glass container with a lid. Screw the lid on tight, and shake well to combine.
2. Add as many washcloths as you can fit into the container. You should be able to fit at least 6 regular-sized washcloths. Old cut-up towels and T-shirts also work well. Replace the lid, and shake again to wet the cloths.
3. To use, remove a cloth, wring out the excess cleaning liquid back into the container, and wipe surfaces clean. When the washcloths get dirty, launder with other cleaning towels, and reuse.

**321** **Clean and disinfect bath toys with a vinegar soak.** Fill a bucket or sink with water, and add ½ cup of white vinegar per 1 gallon of water. Soak the toys for 15–20 minutes, then scrub with a clean sponge or cloth. Rinse well, and lay on a towel to dry.

**322** **Use body wash to reduce soap scum buildup.** Washing with body wash instead of soap will reduce soap scum buildup in your shower or bathtub.

**323** **Zap mold from around the tub without scrubbing using hydrogen peroxide and a cotton beauty coil.** Soak a cotton beauty coil (used for perms) in hydrogen peroxide, and lay it on moldy caulking around the top of the tub. Let it sit overnight, then rinse. The mold will be gone!

**324** **Scrape away soap scum with a putty knife.** Use a plastic putty knife to remove soap scum from shower walls and doors without scratching.

325 **Eliminate soap scum from shower doors with natural hair spray.** Spray shower doors with hair spray, wait for 5 minutes, then rinse with soap and water to remove soap scum with ease.

326 **Remove water stains from shower glass with shaving cream.** Apply shaving cream to glass surfaces in your shower. Let it sit for 15–20 minutes, then wipe with a cloth.

327 **Use a squeegee to wipe water from shower walls.** Wipe shower walls and doors with a squeegee after every use to remove moisture that may encourage mold and bacteria growth.

328 **Whiten grout with baking soda and hydrogen peroxide.** Sprinkle grout with baking soda, and spray liberally with hydrogen peroxide. Let the mixture bubble for a few minutes, then scrub with a brush or old toothbrush and wipe clean.

**329** **Remove bathtub rings naturally with a grapefruit.** Dip ½ of a cut grapefruit in salt, and use it to remove bathtub rings in record time! The citric acid in grapefruit cuts through dirt and soap scum, and salt works as an abrasive to scrub away even the toughest stains. Squeeze out the grapefruit juice as you scrub for even more cleaning power.

**330** **Scrub your bathroom without hurting your arm by using a drill.** Buy a brush to attach to your drill, and let it do all the scrubbing for you!

**331** **Whiten shower tiles with hydrogen peroxide.** Wipe the shower dry with a towel, then spray liberally with hydrogen peroxide. Let it sit for 10–15 minutes, then scrub tiles and grout clean with a brush, scrub sponge, or toothbrush.

**332** **Clean and sanitize with all-natural home-made bleach alternative.** This DIY bleach alternative will clean and disinfect all your bathroom surfaces without the health dangers of chlorine bleach. Plus, it's incredibly cheap to make with just three simple ingredients.

1½ cups hydrogen peroxide

½ cup lemon juice

12 cups water

1-gallon glass jar or jug

1. Mix the ingredients in a 1-gallon glass jar or jug, and stir gently to combine.
2. Put the solution in a spray bottle, and spray surfaces liberally. Let it sit for a few minutes to work its magic, then wipe or rinse clean. You can use this solution to clean all over your bathroom. This recipe will last several months when stored in a cool, dark place.

**333** **Use clear nail polish to stop rust.** Paint that rusty shaving cream can with clear nail polish to stop the rust from transferring to other areas. Let the polish dry before putting the can back in the shower.

**334 Nix hard-water stains from tub jets without scrubbing.** Fill your tub with hot water, making sure to cover the jets completely. Add ½ cup of washing soda and 1 cup of hydrogen peroxide or white vinegar. Run the jets for 10–15 minutes, then let it sit for 1–2 hours. Empty the tub, and refill with cool water. Run the jets again for around 10 minutes, then drain.

**335 Store shaving cream upside down to prevent rust stains.** If you keep your shaving cream in the shower or on the bathroom counter, you may struggle with rust messes caused by the metal can reacting with the moisture in the bathroom. To prevent these rust stains, turn the can upside down, and store it on its plastic cap.

**336 Scrub away rust stains with cream of tartar.** When metal containers rust, they can leave a mess on your sink or tub. To remove the stain, mix 1 tablespoon of cream of tartar with ¼ cup of baking soda, then add hydrogen peroxide to form a thick paste. Apply the paste to the rust spot, and let it sit for 20–30 minutes. Scrub, and rinse clean.

**337** **Add some natural aromatherapy to your shower with fresh eucalyptus.** Grab some fresh eucalyptus from your local florist or garden center, and hang it on your showerhead to make your bathroom smell amazing. The heat and steam from your shower will release calming and therapeutic natural oils in the eucalyptus that can also relieve cold and cough symptoms.

**338** **Give mirrors a streak-free shine with vodka.** Spray straight vodka on mirrors, and wipe clean with a microfiber cloth, paper towels, or strips of paper bags. This method also works great on windows. Don't have any vodka on hand? You can also use hydrogen peroxide or a 50/50 mixture of white vinegar and water. You may have heard that newspaper is a great lint-free way to clean mirrors and windows, but brown paper bags and coffee filters are actually better choices.

**339** **Disinfect toothbrushes with hydrogen peroxide.** You should replace toothbrushes every 3 months or after illness, but you can also disinfect your toothbrush in between replacing by soaking for 5 minutes in hydrogen peroxide. This also works for mouth guards and retainers. Rinse well with water before use.

# 340 **Prevent foggy mirrors with shaving cream.**

To keep bathroom mirrors from fogging after a shower or bath, put a protective layer of shaving cream on your bathroom mirror, then buff dry with paper towels or newspaper to remove streaks. This protective barrier should last several weeks. Don't have shaving cream in the house? You can also use a 50/50 mixture of white vinegar and water. Spray it on your mirror, and buff with paper towels or brown paper bags for a streak-free shine. This should last several days.

# 341 **Defog mirrors quickly with a hair dryer.** Is your mirror already fogged up? You can remove fog by drying your mirror with a hair dryer. Then, use one of the previously mentioned preventative strategies to prevent fog the next time you shower.

# 342 **Use a broom to make scouring the bathtub so much easier.** Do you have trouble bending over to scour the tub? Use a clean broom and some DIY scouring paste or Sal Suds to get the tub sparkling clean without the workout! Bottle brushes and dish wands typically used in the kitchen also work great for this purpose.

**343 Soak grime away from clear plastic faucet handles with vinegar.** To clean clear faucet handles, you'll need to take them apart. Carefully pop the cover off the top of the handle with a flat-head screwdriver to access the screw underneath. Remove the screw with a Phillips-head screwdriver, and disassemble the handle. Soak the handle in white vinegar for 10 minutes, then scrub grime away with a toothbrush. Use cotton swabs to reach into tiny crevices, then rinse well. Clean the faucet and the base of the handles with scouring paste or cleaning spray, and rinse. Make sure everything is completely dry before reassembling.

**344 Hide a chipped tile with matching nail polish.** Paint a chipped tile with nail polish that matches the color of the tile. The small brush will ensure accuracy in even the smallest chips.

**345 Bend your toilet paper roll to prevent unraveling and waste.** Bend your toilet paper roll into an oval shape to keep kids and pets from releasing too much and wasting paper.

# 346 Soak toilet siphons in vinegar to keep your toilet clean longer.

Toilet siphons are the holes under the rim that water runs through when you flush. Clean your toilet bowl as you normally would, making sure to scrub the siphons under the rim. Next, shut off the water to the toilet using the knob behind the toilet. Flush the toilet 2 or 3 times to empty the water tank, then pour a bucket of water into the bowl to completely empty the toilet. Dry under the rim, and cover each siphon with a piece of duct tape. Lift the flapper inside the water tank, and pour white vinegar to fill the rim. Allow it to sit overnight. The next morning, remove the tape, and flush the toilet a few times.

# 347 Prevent toilet hardware from rusting with clear nail polish.

Paint your toilet screws and chrome with a layer of clear nail polish to keep them from flaking and rusting.

# 348 Create a DIY toilet cleaner with germ-fighting hydrogen peroxide. You'll be amazed by how well simple baking soda and vodka can clean your toilet! (This and all the toilet cleaning hacks in this book are safe for septic systems.)

½ cup baking soda

⅓ cup natural dish soap

¼ cup vodka

30 drops eucalyptus or tea tree oil

¾ cup water

Squeeze bottle

1  Mix the ingredients in a squeeze bottle. To use, squirt cleaner around the toilet bowl and scrub.
2  Let it sit for 20 minutes before flushing.

# 349 Scour the toilet with cola. Pour a can of cola or other soft drink in the toilet bowl. Let it sit for an hour, scrub, and flush clean. The acid content and carbonation in the soda help remove dirt and hard-water buildup quickly and easily.

# 350 Make your own natural toilet bombs for hands-off cleaning convenience.

¼ cup citric acid

1 cup baking soda

1 tablespoon natural dish soap

Silicone or plastic ice cube trays

1. Stir the ingredients well to combine in a bowl. Spoon the mixture into silicone ice cube trays, press to tightly pack into cleaning tablets, and level off at the top of the mold. You can also use regular plastic ice cube trays if that's what you have.
2. Let them dry overnight, then pop them out of the mold. Store in an airtight container, such as a 1-quart glass Mason jar.
3. Toss a bomb into the toilet, and let it work its magic. If your toilet isn't very dirty, just flush once the fizzing stops, or you can brush the bowl to remove stains.

# 351 Remove toilet rings with vodka. Pour ½ cup of vodka in your toilet bowl at least once a month to clean and prevent toilet rings. Also, wipe the seat with vodka to clean and disinfect.

352 **Save water with a soda bottle.** If you have an older toilet that doesn't have water-saving features, use this quick tip to save water. Fill an empty 2-liter soda bottle with water, and place it in your toilet tank. This will cause the tank to fill up with less water.

353 **Remove mineral deposits from your water tank with vinegar.** Cleaning your toilet tank regularly—at least twice a year—can extend your toilet's life and make the bowl easier to clean. Shut off the water by turning the knob behind the toilet, then flush 2–3 times to empty the water tank. Remove the lid from the water tank so you can see when the water empties from the tank and can assess how dirty it is. If the tank is mildly grimy, just scrub it clean with an all-purpose spray or baking soda and a scrub brush or sponge. If you have mineral buildup in the tank, you'll need to take some extra steps. Fill the tank up to the overflow valve with white vinegar. This may take 2–3 gallons depending on the size of your tank. Let it sit without flushing for 12 hours, then flush 2–3 times to remove the vinegar from the tank. Scrub the tank with an all-purpose spray or baking soda, and rinse with a bucketful of water to remove the cleaner. If you use baking soda to clean the water tank, rinse and dissolve it with vinegar after scrubbing to help remove it from the tank. Once the toilet is cleaned, turn the water back on, and use as normal.

**354 Prevent your toilet from sweating with Bubble Wrap.** Turn off the water valve, and remove the toilet tank lid. Flush 2–3 times to empty the tank, then line the empty tank with Bubble Wrap. The extra insulation will stop condensation by keeping the outside of the tank from getting too cold.

**355 Keep your toilet clean without scrubbing.** Fill a 16-ounce Mason jar with white vinegar, and punch 3 small holes in the lid with a nail. Place the jar upside down in your toilet's water tank. Every time you flush, a little vinegar will seep out and freshen your toilet. Refill with vinegar about every 3 weeks.

**356 Nix stubborn hard-water stains from your toilet with borax and vinegar.** Pour ½ cup of borax in the toilet bowl, and use a toilet brush to distribute the powder evenly throughout the bowl. Add ½ cup of white vinegar, and let it sit for 30 minutes. Scrub away hard-water stains with the toilet brush, then flush.

357 **Clear toilet clogs with boiling water.** Fill a medium saucepan with water, and bring it to a boil. Carefully pour the boiling water into the toilet bowl to dissolve the clog.

358 **Clean your plunger with dish soap and hydrogen peroxide.** Add a squirt of dish soap and ½ cup of hydrogen peroxide to the toilet bowl. Swirl your plunger around the bowl, then flush.

359 **Use baby oil to polish porcelain easily.** You don't need to use toxic commercial porcelain polish to make your bathroom shine. Put a few drops of baby oil on a cloth, and polish sinks and toilet bowls until the porcelain feels dry. Don't polish showers and tubs, since the oil may make the surface slick and unsafe.

360 **Hang your toilet brush to dry before storing to avoid bacteria.** Put the handle of the toilet brush between the rim and the toilet seat so the brush can drip-dry over the bowl.

**361** **Clean tight spaces at the base of the toilet with your vacuum's crevice tool.** Use the crevice tool to reach into tight spaces a broom can't reach, and suck up dust and hair instantly.

**362** **Keep your toilet brush fresher with vinegar.** Pour some white vinegar in your toilet brush holder to disinfect the brush and neutralize bathroom odors. You can also use vodka or hydrogen peroxide.

**363** **Close the lid on your toilet to keep your bathroom cleaner.** When you flush the toilet without closing the lid first, you're spreading dangerous germs all over your bathroom! Make sure everyone in your family knows to close the lid every time.

**364** **Clean and sanitize makeup brushes with Castile soap and hydrogen peroxide.** Rinse makeup brushes, and wash with a small squirt of liquid Castile soap. Use your hands to scrub away makeup, dirt, and oil. To sanitize, soak brushes in hydrogen peroxide for 5 minutes, then rinse thoroughly, squeeze out excess water, and air-dry.

# 365 Avoid infections by throwing away old beauty
**products.** Using old, expired cosmetics can cause bacterial infections, inflammation, and allergic skin reactions. Go through your products regularly to check your expiration dates and ensure you're not using anything that could harm your health. Here's how long these products should last.

## Less Than 2 Months
○ Shower poufs and loofahs (3 weeks)
○ Sponges (7 weeks)

## 2 to 3 Months
○ Mascara
○ Liquid eyeliner
○ Acne pads
○ Face masks and peels
○ Nonmetal nail files

## 6 Months to a Year
○ Lip gloss (6 months)
○ Lipstick (1 year)
○ Liquid foundation
○ Concealer
○ Face wash
○ Eye cream
○ Acne cleansers and creams
○ Skin serums

### 1 to 1½ Years

- ○ Cream eye shadow
- ○ Eyebrow gel
- ○ Bar soap and body wash
- ○ Sunscreen
- ○ Face cream (in a jar)

### 2 Years

- ○ Powder eye shadow and blush
- ○ Powder foundation
- ○ Nail polish
- ○ Lip and eye pencils
- ○ Body scrubs
- ○ Body lotion (in a jar)

### 3 Years

- ○ Hair spray
- ○ Perfume
- ○ Shampoo and conditioner
- ○ Body lotion (in a pump)

## 366 **Brighten floors with hydrogen peroxide.** Add ½ cup of hydrogen peroxide to 1 gallon of hot water. Use the solution to mop tile and laminate floors to make them bright and clean.

# 367 Use shampoo to clean hairbrushes.

Remove the hair from your hairbrush by raking a comb through the bristles. Rinse the brush in the sink with warm water, then add a drop of shampoo to the bristles. Use your hand to distribute the shampoo, then scrub away dirt and oil with an unused toothbrush. Rinse well under the faucet, soak up excess water with a towel, then allow to air-dry completely before using. Use this method to deep clean your hairbrushes at least once a month.

# 368 Clean hairstyling tools with a DIY cleaning paste.

Hairstyling products can collect on your curling iron and flat iron, forming a burned-on mess that can make them difficult to use—and may be a potential fire hazard! To remove product buildup, make a paste with 1 part rubbing alcohol and 2 parts baking soda. Turn on your styling tools for about a minute, then shut them off. Apply the paste to your hot tools, being careful not to burn your skin, and let them sit for 10 minutes. For ceramic tools, use your finger to remove the buildup so you don't scratch the surface. For metal, use a soft cloth to scrub clean. Once the buildup is loosened, wipe your tools with a wet microfiber cloth, and dry with a clean cloth.

**369** **Use nail polish remover and natural hair spray to clean up nail polish spills.** Clean the spill as quickly as possible to keep the stain from setting. Pour nail polish remover on the spill, let it sit for 1–2 minutes, then wipe it up with paper towels. Scrub the spot with a damp cloth or sponge. If the stain is still there, spray it liberally with hair spray, and let it sit for 5 minutes. Wipe clean with a damp cloth or paper towels. Once the stain is gone, clean the area with soapy water or an all-purpose spray.

**370** **Eliminate urine stains and odors with vinegar, lemon juice, and baking soda.** This is a pretty messy job, so you may want to wear rubber gloves. Mix ¼ cup of lemon juice and enough baking soda to form a thick paste. Apply the paste on urine stains on and around your toilet, including on and under the seat and the floor around the toilet. Pour ½ cup of white vinegar into the toilet tank, and let both sit for 20 minutes. Using a toothbrush dipped in vinegar, scrub the urine messes pretreated with paste. Pour extra vinegar on the paste to dissolve the baking soda, then wipe clean with a cloth. Flush the toilet 2–3 times to remove the vinegar from the tank.

## Natural Ways to Deal with Bathroom Odors

Bathroom odors are an unfortunate reality—but there are lots of easy, inexpensive, and nontoxic ways to address them.

### 371 Banish bathroom odors with homemade "poo" spray. Keep your bathroom smelling fresh and clean with this DIY toilet spray.

1 teaspoon rubbing alcohol

20 drops lemon essential oil

10+ drops essential oil of your choice (lavender and peppermint oils are both great choices)

Water

Mini spray bottle

1. Add the alcohol and essential oil to your spray bottle, then fill with water.
2. Spray the toilet bowl before you go to keep your bathroom smelling clean.

## 372 Keep your trash can fresh with baking soda.

Sprinkle the bottom of your trash can with baking soda to keep odors at bay. For a nice fragrance, add 5–10 drops of your favorite essential oil per ½ cup of baking soda before sprinkling.

## 373 Get a burst of fragrance every time you go.

Put a few drops of your favorite essential oil on the cardboard center of your toilet paper roll to make your bathroom smell great every time you use it.

## 374 Neutralize odors with baking soda. Keep a

small dish of baking soda near the toilet to help neutralize offending odors. Replace every 30 days. To discard, pour the baking soda in the toilet, and flush to freshen the toilet bowl and clean the pipes below.

## 375 Remove tough odors with essential oils. For

really tough odors, or just to make your bathroom smell extra fresh and clean, keep an essential oil burner in your bathroom. Run your essential oil burner when you're expecting guests to make your home even more inviting.

# CLEARING BATHROOM DRAINS

**376** **Make a DIY wire hook to clear stopped drains.**
Unfold an old wire clothes hanger to make a long wire.
Using pliers, bend the end of the wire to form a hook. Put
on protective gloves. Remove the drain cover and any
dirt, hair, and other debris you can reach with your hand,
then use the hook to fish out anything you can't reach.

**377** **Clean slow-moving drains with salt and water.**
Add 1 cup of salt to boiling water or superhot tap water,
and pour the mixture down the drain to break down soap
clogs.

**378** **Keep drains clear with boiling water.** To keep
pipes clear, pour a pot of boiling water down your drains
once per week. This method works best on metal pipes
since boiling water may be too hot for PVC pipes. If you
don't have metal pipes, use the hottest water from your
tap.

# 379 Clear deep clogs with a drain snake.

Use a drain snake, available at hardware stores and online, to clear drains like the pros. To use, slowly insert the snake into the drain. Once you get it down deep into the drain, slowly twist it around a few times to gather the hair and debris that are clogging your drain, then pull the snake back up and out of the drain. Remove the mess from the snake, and repeat the steps 2–3 more times to make sure you've removed the entire clog.

# 380 Prevent clogs with a hair filter.

Install a hair filter in the shower drain to keep hair from going down the drain. As the hair gathers in the filter, just pick it up, and throw it in the trash.

## Effective Ways to Get Rid of Mold and Mildew

When cleaning mold, wear a face mask and gloves, especially if you're sensitive to mold, mildew, and other allergens, to prevent health problems from mold exposure.

**381 Run the exhaust fan to prevent mold.** Mold isn't just unsightly—it's also a potentially serious health hazard that's common in wet areas of the home, including bathrooms. To prevent mold and mildew from forming in your bathroom, make it a rule to always run the exhaust fan every time you take a shower or bath to remove steam and moisture that can help bacteria grow. You can also increase air circulation by opening a window and running a dehumidifier.

**382 Clean mold, grime, and hard-water deposits from the base of the faucet with a vinegar soak.** Saturate a paper towel or cleaning cloth with white vinegar, and wrap it around the base of the faucet to remove bacteria, grime, and mold. Let it sit for 30 minutes to an hour, wipe, and then rinse clean.

**383 Prevent mold and mildew on the shower curtain with a salt bath.** Take down your shower curtain, and soak it in a tub of warm water with ¼ cup of salt. Leave for 3–4 hours or overnight, if possible. The salt creates a protective barrier that helps keep soap scum, mold, and mildew from forming.

## 384 Prevent soap scum with an all-natural homemade daily shower spray.

Spray your shower with this DIY spray every day after your family is finished showering to prevent soap scum, mold, and mildew before it forms.

1½ cups water

1 cup white vinegar

½ cup vodka or rubbing alcohol

1 teaspoon natural dish soap

15 drops lime essential oil

15 drops tea tree oil

1-quart spray bottle

1. Combine the ingredients in a 1-quart spray bottle.
2. Spray on shower doors and walls after every shower.

## 385 Store towels on towel bars to dry completely between uses.

Hooks may seem like an inexpensive and space-saving solution to dry your towels between uses, but it's actually really difficult for towels to dry completely when they're folded up on hooks, which can encourage mildew and bacteria growth.

# 386 Eliminate tough mold stains with a home-made mold eliminator.

This recipe can be used to clean porcelain, tile, and painted walls. If this method doesn't work, you may need to call a mold removal company.

2 cups water

1 cup white vinegar

¼ cup borax

Spray bottle

1. Mix the ingredients in a spray bottle. Shake well to combine, then spray the affected area liberally with the solution.
2. Scrub with a brush or sponge, and wipe clean with a cloth or paper towels.
3. Spray again, let it sit for 10–15 minutes, then wipe clean.

# 387 Remove grime and mildew in hard-to-reach places with an old toothbrush.

Use a toothbrush to scrub mildew away from faucet bases, grout, and other places cleaning cloths just can't reach.

# 388 Nix mold and mildew from your shower with vodka.

Spray vodka on the area, and let it sit for 10–15 minutes. Scrub with a brush or sponge, then rinse clean.

# 6. LAUNDRY

Store-bought laundry products usually contain myriad fragrances and chemicals. These cost a lot of money, can irritate skin, and don't always work as promised. Use the easy tips in this chapter to get your laundry sparkling clean—for a fraction of the cost!

# 389

**Make your own washing soda for cents.** If you're in a pinch and can't run out to get washing soda, you can make your own at home with almost no effort. Heat your oven to 400°F. Sprinkle a layer (½ inch thick) of baking soda on a cookie sheet, and bake for about 1 hour, stirring occasionally. You'll know it's done by the way it looks. Baking soda likes to clump together, while washing soda is dryer and grainier. Let it cool, and store in an airtight jar.

# 390

**Whip up DIY natural laundry pods for grab-and-go convenience.** Now you can have the convenience of laundry pods without the dangerous chemicals in commercial brands! Take 2 cups of the DIY laundry powder described later in this chapter (or any natural laundry powder), and spray it with white vinegar until just damp enough to hold together when you squeeze it in your hand. Spoon a heaping tablespoon into each compartment of a square silicone mold. Pack it down into the mold with your fingers, and level it off at the top. If you don't have a silicone mold, a regular plastic ice cube tray is fine. Let the tablets dry for 12–24 hours, then pop them out of the mold. Use 1 pod per load for front-loading machines and HE top-loading machines and 2 pods for regular top-loading machines and large loads.

# 391 Save money by making your own all-natural laundry powder. Clean your clothes, bedding, and more with this natural and effective DIY laundry powder at a fraction of the cost of store-bought laundry detergents. This DIY recipe is safe to use in high-efficiency (HE) washing machines.

1 bar of natural soap (I like Castile soap)

1 cup washing soda

1 cup borax

Airtight container for storage

1. Grate the bar of soap with a cheese grater or food processor into a medium-sized bowl. Transfer the soap into an airtight storage container, such as a 1-quart glass Mason jar. Add the washing soda and borax, and shake or stir to mix well.

2. Use 1 tablespoon for small loads or 2–3 tablespoons for large or heavily soiled loads. This recipe yields approximately 32 ounces of laundry powder, so it will last for about 32–64 loads (depending on how much you use per load).

## 392 Mix up an all-natural liquid laundry soap

**for pennies.** Do you prefer to use liquid laundry soap instead of powder? Here's an easy DIY liquid laundry soap that is just as cheap and effective as powder soap and is safe to use in HE washers.

5 cups water, divided

1 cup washing soda

¾ cup Sal Suds

2 (1-quart) glass jars

1. Bring the water to a boil. Put the washing soda in a large glass bowl, and slowly pour 3 cups of the boiling water over the washing soda. Mix well with a whisk until the washing soda is completely dissolved.
2. Add the Sal Suds, and mix well. Then mix in the rest of the water. Store the laundry soap in a couple of 1-quart glass jars, and use ¼ to ½ cup of soap per load. If the soap separates, just shake it to combine.

## 393 Use washing soda as a natural laundry

**booster.** Add ½ cup to laundry (in addition to another laundry cleanser) to clean, brighten, and deodorize.

**394** **Make a "right away" bin for your laundry room to quickly prioritize really dirty clothes.** Throw sweaty, stained, or smelly items in there, and wash as soon as possible. You're more likely to get the stains out, and that will make clothes last longer.

**395** **Cut down on sorting time by washing family members' clothes separately.** Wash everyone's clothes in separate loads so you don't have to spend extra time sorting clothes. If your kids are old enough, you can even make them responsible for laundering their own clothing. Give everyone a set day to wash their clothes to help avoid arguments. You'll be teaching them an important life skill and free up some much-needed time for yourself.

**396** **Prevent lice by using tea tree oil in the laundry.** Add a few drops of tea tree oil in the wash to help your child fend off lice during the school year. (You can also add a few drops to their shampoo.)

## How Often Should You Do Your Laundry?

If you wash your clothes too much, they may wear out faster, plus it will cost you money on higher energy bills (electric, gas, water) and replacement clothes. This guide shows how often you should wash your clothing with typical use.

### Every Wear
- ○ Shirts
- ○ Blouses
- ○ White clothes
- ○ Underwear
- ○ Bathing suits
- ○ Workout clothes

### Every 3 Wears/Uses
- ○ Bras
- ○ Pants, jeans, and shorts
- ○ Sweatshirts and sweaters
- ○ Suits
- ○ Dresses
- ○ Hand towels
- ○ Washcloths
- ○ Bath towels

### Every Week
- ○ Dish towels
- ○ Cleaning towels/cloths
- ○ Bedsheets
- ○ Bath mats

### Every Month
- ○ Throw blankets
- ○ Throw rugs
- ○ Bathrobes
- ○ Pillow covers

### Every 3 Months
- ○ Outerwear
- ○ Mattress pads/covers
- ○ Shower curtains

### Every 6 Months
- ○ Comforter
- ○ Pillows

397 **Store liquid laundry soap in a 1-gallon jar with spout for easy access.** Put homemade or store-bought liquid laundry soap in a glass beverage container with a leak-free spout, and store it on an easy-to-reach shelf in your laundry room to make dispensing quick and easy.

398 **Wash new clothes before wearing to avoid skin irritation.** New clothes are coated in dangerous chemicals from the manufacturing process, so be sure to wash your new clothes before wearing them for the first time to keep harmful chemicals and dyes off your skin.

399 **Keep colors from running with vinegar.** Add ½ cup of white vinegar to the wash to keep colors from running.

400 **Don't overload the washer to clean clothes more efficiently.** Keep loads to a manageable size to allow water and laundry soaps to work. The same goes for the dryer. Your washer and dryer can even last longer without the added stress of oversized loads.

**401** **Wash delicates in a mesh laundry bag to prevent tangles.** Put delicate clothes like blouses, pantyhose and tights, bras, and lingerie in mesh laundry bags to protect them and keep them from getting damaged in the wash. You can find mesh bags for delicates at department stores, big-box stores, and online.

**402** **Use a laundry bag to keep socks paired.** Tired of losing socks in the wash? Have each family member put their socks in a small mesh laundry bag. Toss the bags in the washer, and then wash and dry as usual to make pairing socks a cinch.

**403** **Stop static cling with natural hair spray.** Spray clothes with hair spray to eliminate static cling instantly.

**404** **Fix static cling on your pants with a safety pin.** Hide a safety pin near the hem of your pants. The extra weight will make static cling go away.

## Chemical-Free Ways to Keep Jeans from Fading

Keep your jeans looking newer longer with these easy tips.

**405** **Wash correctly.** Launder jeans inside out using the gentle cycle and cold water to help preserve their color. Wash with other jeans, if possible, so that if some color does leach out, it will adhere to the jeans instead of other garments.

**406** **Do laundry less often.** Most people launder their clothes more often than they need to. Unless you have an active, dirty job or do lots of grimy household chores, you can probably wear jeans several times before washing. If your jeans are smelling a little funky but aren't dirty, put them in a sealable 1-gallon bag, and pop them in the freezer for at least 30 minutes to an hour to kill odor-causing bacteria without running through the wash.

**407** **Spot-treat stains.** Instead of tossing jeans in the wash every time they get a little dirty, spot-treat them when you can. Spray ink stains with natural hair spray, then blot with a cloth to remove. For grease stains, put a tiny dab of natural dish soap on a white cloth, and use it to gently rub the stain away.

**408** **Hang to dry out of the sun.** To keep colors brighter longer, hang them outside to dry out of direct sunlight or indoors on a clothes-drying rack. This will also keep them from shrinking.

**409** **Soften hard water with washing soda.** Add ½ cup of washing soda to laundry to soften hard water. Softening hard water helps you save money on laundry since you can use less laundry soap and prevent costly washing machine repairs caused by limescale buildup.

**410** **Save money with a DIY stain remover.** Combine 1 part natural dish soap with 2 parts hydrogen peroxide in a dark-colored spray bottle. (Hydrogen peroxide is sensitive to light, so storing in a dark bottle will keep it from losing its potency.) Shake gently to combine, and spray the solution directly on stains. Let them sit for 5–10 minutes, then wash as usual. For really tough stains, spray liberally, and let them sit overnight before washing.

**411** **Use vinegar as an inexpensive, all-natural fabric softener.** Vinegar naturally softens fabrics and has the added benefit of removing detergent buildup and odors. Put some white vinegar in a Downy Ball or add to your washer's fabric softener dispenser. Use ½ cup in regular washers to ¾ cup for large loads, and use ¼ cup in HE washers. Don't worry about the vinegar making your clothes smell—that smell will dissipate once clothes are dry. You can also add essential oils to the vinegar to freshen clothes.

# Simple Ways to Remove Tough Stains

Treat stains as soon as possible for a better chance of completely removing them. Clothes dryers set stains, making them more difficult or even impossible to get out. When trying to remove stains, air-dry the garment after washing to ensure the stain is completely gone. Once the stain is out, wash and dry as usual.

**412** **Treat tough stains and odors with a presoak.** Start your washer. Once it fills with water, stop the cycle, and add 1 cup of washing soda. Let the clothes soak for 20 minutes before starting the washer to finish the cleaning cycle.

**413** **Soak up oil stains with powder.** To remove a tough oil stain, spray stain remover on the garment, then sprinkle with diatomaceous earth, cornstarch, or arrowroot powder. The powder will absorb the stain. Let it sit for 10–15 minutes, then wash as usual.

**414** **Remove ink, oil, makeup, and even dried paint stains with natural hair spray.** Spray stains liberally, let them sit for 5–10 minutes, then wash as usual. For paint stains, saturate the stain with hair spray, then rub the fabric with a butter knife, or a soft-bristled toothbrush for delicate fabrics, to loosen the stain. Run warm water on the stain to wash away the loosened paint. Keep repeating these steps until the paint is gone.

**415** **Use hydrogen peroxide to remove armpit stains.** Mix 1 part dish soap with 2 parts hydrogen peroxide. Apply the solution to the sweat stain, and let it sit for 1 hour. Wash as usual.

**416** **Scrape away paint stains with a razor.** Allow the paint to dry, then scrape it off clothing fibers with a razor blade, being careful not to cut yourself or the fabric.

**417** **Remove grease and other tough stains with washing soda.** Sprinkle washing soda directly on the stain, and wash immediately. Don't allow undiluted washing soda to sit on clothes, as it can eat through fabrics and fade colors due to its high alkalinity.

**418** **Pretreat makeup stains with shaving cream.** Did you accidentally rub some foundation on your collar? Squirt some shaving cream on the stain and let it sit for 5 minutes. Wash as usual.

**419** **Keep colors bright with black pepper.** Add a teaspoon of black pepper to the wash to brighten colors and prevent fading. Colors usually fade due to detergent buildup. Black pepper works as an abrasive to remove dirt and detergent from clothes.

**420 Use a crayon to free a caught zipper.** Color a caught zipper with a crayon. Use a crayon that's the same color as the zipper. The zipper will move freely along the track, and the crayon won't stain your clothes like oil can.

**421 Remove gum from clothes with an ice cube.** Put an ice cube on the gum to freeze it hard, then scrape it out of the fabric. You can also pop the garment in the freezer to get the same effect.

**422 Use vinegar to clean your washer almost effortlessly.** To clean front-loading washing machines, fill the dispenser with white vinegar, set to hot water and largest load, and run the cycle. Use the cleaning cycle if your washer has that option. For newer top-loading machines, use the cleaning cycle, if available, or the normal cycle if your machine doesn't have that option. Fill the dispenser with vinegar, and run the cycle. For older top-loading machines, fill with hot water, and add 3 cups of white vinegar. Let it sit for 30 minutes, then turn it on to run through the normal cycle. For all machines: Once the cycle is finished, scrub the drum with a cloth or sponge. Use a toothbrush to get into hard-to-reach spaces. Be sure to clean well around the seals to remove soap scum and mildew.

## Surprising Things You Can Clean in the Washing Machine

Maybe the best cleaning hack of all is not having to do any of the work at all! Let the washer do the cleaning for you! You might be surprised by what you can throw in the washing machine:

**423** **Stuffed animals.** Place each stuffed animal in its own mesh laundry bag. Wash with cold water and ½ the usual amount of laundry soap. Do a second rinse if any soap remains on the toy, then air-dry. Fluff fur with your hands or a dry towel, if needed.

**424** **Pet supplies.** Throw small pet beds, collars, leashes, and toys right in the washing machine. Use laundry bags as needed. Air-dry toys, collars, and leashes. Air-dry beds, or toss them in the dryer with dryer balls or tennis balls to fluff up the filling. Is your pet's bed too large to fit in the washer or dryer? Hand-wash it in the bathtub with Sal Suds or laundry soap. Rinse well, then air-dry. Wash sturdy items in hot water to kill even more germs. Use warm water to prevent damage to more delicate items.

**425** **Pillows.** Clean machine washable pillows in the washing machine following care label instructions. Wash two pillows at once to help the washer stay balanced. Dry in the dryer with dryer balls or tennis balls to fluff them back up.

**426** **Sports gear.** Close Velcro closures to prevent tangles. Throw sports gear, including gloves (nonleather), shin guards, and pads (elbow, knee, and shoulder), into the washer with ½ the usual amount of laundry soap, then air-dry.

**427** **Plastic shower curtain liners.** Put your shower curtain liner in the washer. Add your laundry soap and 1 cup of baking soda, then add a few towels to help scrub away soap scum and mildew and keep the curtain from ripping. Wash in warm water to prevent the curtain from melting. Once the wash cycle ends, immediately remove the liner and hang it back up in the shower to dry.

**428** **Window curtains.** You can wash lace, sheer, and other light curtains in the washing machine on the gentle cycle using cold water. Put delicate lace or sheer curtains in a mesh laundry bag or pillowcase before laundering. (Heavy or velvet curtains can't be cleaned in the washing machine.)

**429** **Baseball hats.** The best way to clean ball caps is to put them in a cap washer before tossing in the washing machine. If you don't use a cap washer, you run the risk of ruining the shape of the cap and its comfortable fit. If you don't have a cap washer, which you can find online or in big-box stores, you can also throw them in the top rack of the dishwasher. Run them in their own cycle, then clean your dishwasher by running an additional empty cycle before using for dishes.

**430 Shower poufs and loofahs.** Put shower poufs and loofahs in a mesh laundry bag or pillowcase, and toss in the washer with a load of towels. Wash in hot water to kill germs. Hang them up in the shower to air-dry.

**431 Bath mats and throw rugs.** Shake rugs and bath mats to remove dirt and debris, then put them in the washer. Distribute them evenly in the washer to keep your washer balanced. Add laundry soap, and wash with cold water. Wash rubber-backed bath mats on the gentle cycle. Throw rugs in the dryer, or air-dry if that's best for the material (always air-dry rubber-backed rugs and mats).

**432 Sneakers.** Canvas shoes and sneakers can also be cleaned up in the washing machine. Remove the laces, and put them in a mesh laundry bag or pillowcase. Throw the shoes and laundry bag (or pillowcase) in the washer. Use the normal amount of laundry soap, and add ½ cup of white vinegar to remove odors. Wash as usual in warm water, then air-dry.

**433 Yoga mats.** Unless the care instructions advise against it, you should be able to clean your mat in the washing machine. Toss it into the washer, and wash in warm water without soap. Dry in the dryer on medium to high heat. Wash your yoga mat once every 1–2 months.

**434 Hair accessories.** Throw hair ties and head-bands in a mesh laundry bag or pillowcase, and toss it in the washer with other laundry.

435 **Stop static cling with aluminum foil.** Tear off a couple sheets of aluminum foil, and use them to form a ball about 2 to 3 inches in diameter. Throw the ball in the dryer, and run the cycle as usual.

436 **Dry similar-weight items together to decrease drying time.** You shouldn't just separate the wash according to color; it's also helpful to separate items according to type and weight. Wash towels, jeans, and lightweight T-shirts in separate loads. If you dry a T-shirt with towels, it's going to take the T-shirt much longer to dry than if you just did a load of shirts. Plus, you won't get any lint from the towels on your clothing.

# 437 Save time and money with homemade wool dryer balls.

Natural wool dryer balls save money on energy costs because wool dryer balls soften and fluff clothes, reduce static without chemicals, and help clothes dry faster. Plus, unlike dryer sheets, they typically last for 1,000+ loads! How many dryer balls you use really depends on personal preference. You should use at least 4–6 balls to notice a decrease in drying time, and use up to 8 for large loads. I prefer to make my dryer balls out of lightly spun roving yarn because it felts better than tighter yarns, but you can use any 100% wool yarn or even an unspun old sweater, as long as it's 100% wool. If the yarn contains any other material, it won't felt correctly.

2–3 skeins 100% wool yarn (not "superwash" or washable yarn, which won't felt)

Large-eyed felting needle or crochet hook

Scissors

Pantyhose or knee-highs

A cotton or acrylic string to tie the pantyhose (not wool)

1 Wrap the yarn about 10 times around your first two fingers. Hold the yarn together, and pull it off your fingers.

**2** Wrap the yarn around the middle of this little bundle of yarn, and continue wrapping in a circle to form a ball. Once it reaches the desired size (from the size of a tennis ball up to a softball), use the felting needle or crochet hook to tuck the end of the yarn back into the ball through several layers of yarn. Pull the yarn through the ball, and cut the end. You can also save money by filling the ball with an old sock or other fabric instead of making it completely out of wool yarn. Repeat these steps until you have the desired number of balls.

**3** Cut the leg off an old pair of pantyhose, or use knee-highs. Drop your wool balls into the stocking, tying between each ball. Do not use the wool yarn to tie, because it will felt around the pantyhose. You can use cotton thread, acrylic yarn, or even a shoelace.

**4** Throw the balls wrapped in pantyhose in the washer with a load of towels, wash with hot water and a cold-water rinse cycle, and dry on the hottest dryer setting. Unwrap your balls to check for felting. You may need to repeat the washing and drying cycles 3–4 times until the balls are completely felted. You'll know they're done when you run your fingernail along the ball and the strings of yarn no longer separate.

Forget to check just one pocket, and you might have a serious mess on your hands.

**438** **Use laundry soap to clean up clothing dyes.** Make a thick paste with laundry soap and some water, and apply it to the stain. Let it sit for 5–10 minutes, then rub the stain away with a cloth. After the stain is removed, wipe the drum clean with a damp cloth.

**439** **Scrape away gum or candy with an old credit card.** Gently scrape as much of the mess as you can with a plastic putty knife or credit card, being careful not to scratch the coating on the drum. If any mess remains, apply ice for a minute or two. Once the gunk hardens, scrape gently with the putty knife or credit card. For tough messes, pour white vinegar on a cloth, and lay it on the sticky spots for 20–30 minutes. This should loosen up the mess.

**440** **Remove ink and marker stains with vodka.** Spray the vodka liberally on the drum, and wipe or scrub clean with a white cloth or sponge.

**441** **Clean up melted crayon, lipstick, or lip balm with damp towels.** Toss old, damp towels into the dryer, and run the machine on high heat for 5 minutes. This softens the mess, and it will wipe up easily with a few sprays of white vinegar or vodka and a towel. Once the mess is gone, wipe the drum again with a towel dipped in water.

**442** **Make your own cheap and effective all-natural wrinkle-release spray.** This DIY wrinkle releaser is perfect for when you're on the go and don't have the time, or the desire, to break out the electric clothes iron.

2 cups water

2 tablespoons white vinegar

1 teaspoon hair conditioner

Spray bottle

1. Mix the ingredients in a spray bottle, and shake well to combine.
2. Spread the garment out on a flat surface. Shake the bottle again to mix the ingredients, and spray clothes until slightly damp.
3. Smooth the wrinkles, and air-dry.

**443** **Dry delicates with a salad spinner.** For small items of clothing too delicate to go in the dryer, pop them in the salad spinner to remove excess water before laying flat to dry.

**444** **Unshrink clothes with hair conditioner.** Fill a bucket or sink with warm water, add 1 tablespoon of hair conditioner, and stir with your hand to combine. Soak the garment in the mixture for 20–30 minutes. Remove, and gently squeeze excess water out of the fabric. Don't wring, or you may cause wrinkles and odd shapes to form in the fabric. Lay the garment flat on a clean, dry bath towel, then roll it up in the towel and squeeze to remove more moisture to make the item damp instead of wet. Replace the towel with another dry towel, and start stretching the garment back to its original size and shape. Allow to air-dry. To speed up the drying process, either hang outside or set in front of a fan. Air-dry for future washes, as well, to prevent the garment from shrinking again.

**445** **Fluff down after washing with tennis balls.** Throw 2–3 tennis balls in the dryer with down pillows, down coats, and down comforters to fluff them back up after washing.

## Quick Tips for Caring for Your Clothes Iron

Irons need to be maintained just like any other appliance. Follow these tips to make the process easy and fast.

**446** **Wipe clean after every use.** The best way to prevent your iron from requiring a deep cleaning is to wipe it down every time you use it. Let the iron cool completely before cleaning so you don't burn yourself. Spray a cleaning cloth or paper towel lightly with all-purpose spray, and wipe the iron clean, paying special attention to the ironing plate.

**447** **Empty the water reservoir every time.** It may be tempting to leave the water in your iron after use, but this can allow bacteria, mold, and minerals to build up, which can be difficult to clean and may shorten the life of your iron.

**448** **Clean starch from your iron with baking soda.** Form a thick paste with baking soda and distilled water. Dip a white cloth or paper towel into the paste, and use to scrub the soleplate. Wipe the plate clean with a damp microfiber cloth. If any baking soda residue remains, rinse with a little white vinegar, then wipe again with the damp microfiber cloth.

**449** **Iron salt to remove stains and residue from the soleplate.** Pour some salt on a piece of paper, and run your iron over the salt several times to remove stains and residue left behind from ironing clothes. Unplug the iron, and once cooled, wipe it with a clean cloth.

**450** **Unclog a steam iron with vinegar.** Mix ½ cup of white vinegar with ½ cup of distilled water. Use distilled water because the clog is most likely caused by minerals in your tap water. Pour the mixture into a completely cool and unplugged iron. Put the iron in an upright position, and look at the steam ducts in the soleplate. If you see any mineral deposits, clean them with a microfiber cloth or old toothbrush. Turn on the iron, and set it to steam. Once it heats up, press the steam button several times to circulate the vinegar through the steam ducts. Turn off the iron, and let it cool completely. Pour out any remaining vinegar solution, and put away the iron.

**451** **Use ice cubes to remove melted plastic.** Fill a sturdy bowl or pan with ice cubes, place the stained part of the iron on the ice, and let it sit for 10 minutes. Once the plastic hardens from the cold, use a plastic putty knife to remove the plastic, then clean the iron with a thick paste made with baking soda and distilled water. If the melted plastic gets on clothes, put them in the freezer, and use the putty knife to scrape away the hardened plastic.

# KEEPING WHITE CLOTHES BRIGHT

**452** **Keep white laundry separate.** You may not think separating your white laundry is that important, but it only takes one red sock to ruin your favorite white shirt or even an entire load of white clothes. Also, you may not immediately notice when your whites start looking din-gier over time, but they will at some point if you're wash-ing them with dark colors. The best practice is to wash white clothes alone every time. Then you can use the fol-lowing whitening hacks without worrying about harming your colors!

**453** **Whiten laundry with hydrogen peroxide.** Add ½ cup of hydrogen peroxide to a load of laundry to brighten whites.

**454** **Make a DIY laundry booster to help clean.** If your laundry detergent isn't working well enough to remove dirt and stains from white clothes, add 1 cup of baking soda and ½ cup of borax to each load to give it some extra cleaning and whitening power.

**455** **Make your own homemade bleach alternative.** Whiten laundry without the dangers of commercial bleach with this easy three-ingredient DIY bleach alternative. Since this solution is mostly water, it's perfectly fine to use this amount in HE washers too. You can also use this mixture as an all-purpose cleaner all over your house. Do not save any remaining mixture.

1½ cups hydrogen peroxide

½ cup lemon juice

12 cups water

1-gallon glass jar or jug

1 Mix the ingredients in the jar, and stir gently to combine.

2 Add 1–2 cups to each load of whites.

**456** **Use the hottest water recommended on care labels.** Washing white clothes in the hottest water recommended for that fabric will help keep them whiter longer.

**457** **Brighten dull whites with lemon juice.** Pour ½ cup of lemon juice into a load of whites to brighten without dangerous chemicals.

**458** **Use vinegar as a fabric softener.** Commercial fabric softeners can leave residue on clothes, making them appear dull. Add 1 cup of white vinegar to the rinse cycle to remove detergent residues, soften clothes, and leave whites bright.

**459** **Treat stains with hydrogen peroxide.** Pour some hydrogen peroxide on the stain, and let it sit for 10–15 minutes. Blot with a cloth, then rinse in cold water. This even works on bloodstains!

**460** **Use salt to whiten wool.** Fill a sink or bucket with cold water, and toss in ½ cup of salt. Soak the wool sweater or scarf in the solution overnight. The next morning, swish the garment in the water one final time to remove any dirt. Remove from the water, and squeeze as much water out as you can without wringing. Lay it flat to dry.

## 461 Save money with a DIY oxygen bleach.

This homemade oxygen bleach recipe is much cheaper and works just as well as a store-bought kind but without the dangerous chemicals!

1 tablespoon washing soda

1 tablespoon hydrogen peroxide

2 tablespoons water

Spray bottle

1. Mix the ingredients in a bowl. Put in a spray bottle to pretreat stains before washing, or use it to soak laundry.
2. Add the entire mixture to a load of laundry, and fill the washing machine with water. Soak the laundry for 30 minutes, then wash as usual. Only mix as much as you need for immediate use since the mixture quickly loses its effectiveness when stored.

## 462 Use lemon and sunshine to bleach stains naturally.

Put lemon juice on stains, and hang the shirt out in the sun to dry. The sun and lemon will work together to whiten even the toughest stains!

**463** **Whiten pillows with hydrogen peroxide.** Wash 2 pillows at once to help keep your washing machine balanced and facilitate cleaning. Set your washing machine to soak, and add 1 cup of hydrogen peroxide. Run the pillows through the cycle, then toss in the dryer.

**464** **Hang clothes outside to dry.** Make it a habit of drying white clothes outside in the sunshine all the time, not just when they're stained. The ultraviolet rays from the sun will help whiten and brighten garments naturally.

**465** **Use a low heat setting on the dryer.** If you dry your clothes in the dryer, choose the lowest setting for white clothes. High heat can cause whites to turn yellow, and it sets stains.

**466** **Remove stains with salt.** Make a paste with 1 tablespoon of salt and a few drops of water. Rub it into the stain, and let it sit for an hour. Rinse with warm water, and watch the stain disappear!

# REMOVING ODORS

**467** **Remove offensive odors from towels with vinegar and baking soda.** To deep clean towels, fill your washer with hot water, add 1 cup of white vinegar, and run towels through a wash cycle. Once that cycle is complete, leave the towels in the washer. Add ½ cup of baking soda, wash again in hot water, then dry thoroughly in the dryer or outside. The odors should be completely gone, but if any linger, you can repeat this process until your towels smell fresh and clean. Use this method when you notice your towels aren't as fresh and absorbent as usual.

**468** **Nix underarm odors with vodka.** Mix ⅓ cup of vodka and 1 cup of water in a spray bottle, and shake to combine. Perform a spot test on an inconspicuous spot, and if it works okay, spray liberally on smelly underarm fabric on shirts, blouses, and even dry-clean-only garments, and let them sit overnight. Check the garment in the morning. If the smell is still there, re-treat. If the smell is gone, wash the garment in cold water, and hang to dry. The heat from the dryer can set odors if they aren't completely gone. Once you're sure the odors are out of the garment, launder as usual.

**469** **Keep clothes smelling fresh with lavender essential oil.** Do you have a load you need to wash but won't be able to dry immediately? To keep odors at bay, put a couple drops of lavender essential oil or another antifungal oil on a sock or rag, and add it to the wash.

**470** **Soak linens to remove offensive odors.** If your bed linens aren't smelling fresh and clean after washing, soak them in a bucket or sink filled with hot water. Add 1 cup of white vinegar and 1 tablespoon of natural dish soap, and stir the solution with your arm to mix. Add your sheets, and swish them around to saturate them in the cleaning solution. Soak for at least 30 minutes or overnight, then wash as usual.

**471** **Use baking soda to remove tough odors.** Remove even the toughest odors like gasoline from your clothes by soaking them in baking soda. Fill a bucket or the washing machine with warm water, and add 1 cup of baking soda. Soak the smelly garment in the mixture for 3–4 hours or overnight, then launder as usual. Repeat for extreme odors.

## 472 Make a laundry scent booster with salt and essential oil.

You don't need the strong, synthetic fragrances in commercial products to make your laundry smell fresh and clean. This DIY laundry scent booster provides a nice, light fragrance without unhealthy chemicals!

3-pound box kosher salt

25–30 drops essential oil

½-gallon Mason jar

1. Pour the salt in a medium bowl, and add your favorite essential oils, such as lavender, lemongrass, peppermint, or lemon. Stir well to combine. Store the mixture in an airtight container.
2. To use, add ½ cup into the washing machine per load, and launder as usual. The salt will soften clothes, and the essential oil will freshen and remove dirt and odors.

## 473 Scrub away mold and mildew with a toothbrush.

If the garment has visible mold on it, use a toothbrush to gently scrape it away before washing to allow the washing machine to reach deep into the fibers and remove the rest of the stain.

# MILDEW

**474** **Use buttermilk to remove mildew stains from clothes.** Soak the garment for a few hours in 1 cup of buttermilk in 1 gallon of water before washing. The high acid content in the buttermilk will help kill mildew and germs.

**475** **Freshen musty towels with vodka.** Start filling your washer with water, and add ⅓ cup of vodka and the amount of laundry soap you typically use for soiled loads. Once the washer is finished filling with water, add the towels, let them soak for 1–2 hours, then wash as usual. Once the cycle is complete, check to see if the smell is gone, and repeat the process, if necessary.

**476** **Nix mildew smells with vinegar.** Fill your washer's fabric softener dispenser with white vinegar to kill bacteria and neutralize odors in your laundry. You can also put the vinegar in a Downy Ball and toss it in the wash for the same effect.

**477** **Soak laundry with tough mildew odors.** Add 1 cup of white vinegar to a bucket of water. Use warm water unless the clothes label recommends otherwise. (Don't use hot water, since it may set the stain.) Soak clothes for a few hours or overnight, then wash in the morning with additional vinegar added to the fabric softener dispenser.

**478** **Soak with homemade oxygen bleach.** Mix up a batch of DIY oxygen bleach (see earlier in this chapter for the recipe). Add it to a bucket of warm water or a washing machine filled with water, and soak the item until the stain is removed. Some mildew stains will lift quickly, while others will take hours, overnight, or even a few days. Check the stain every hour or two. If you're concerned about colorfastness, check the stain every 20–30 minutes.

**479** **Kill mildew growth with hydrogen peroxide.** For one garment, mix 3 cups of water with ½ cup of hydrogen peroxide, and soak the garment for 15 minutes. Rinse well with water, then wash as usual. Hang to dry outside or in a well-ventilated area.

# 7. BASEMENTS, ATTICS, AND GARAGES

Since these spaces are hidden, it may not seem important to keep them clean, but regularly cleaning your basement, attic, and garage has benefits. You can catch problems with leaks, mold, insulation, pests, and other issues more quickly, and cleaning away dust from these areas will make your whole home cleaner and may improve allergies and asthma symptoms. Finally, storing your belongings in a cleaner place will help them stay in better shape, especially clothing and other fabrics, which can degrade in dirty and moist conditions. Make the job manageable by cleaning these spaces 2–3 times per year.

# BASEMENTS AND ATTICS

480 **Protect yourself.** Since these rooms are often dirty, dusty places, be sure to wear a filtering face mask while you clean to protect your lungs from allergens. Wear gloves to protect your hands from grimy surfaces and sharp objects. In your attic, always walk on floor joists instead of between them to be extra safe.

481 **Move stored items to facilitate easy cleaning.** Stack all your stored belongings in one area, or move things as you go, so you can easily access the floor and other surfaces to clean more thoroughly. Consolidate boxes if you can to reduce clutter and free up more storage containers for use in the rest of the house.

482 **Remove musty smells with an onion.** To remove offensive odors throughout your home, cut an onion in half, and place it near the smell. Let it sit overnight. The onion will absorb the odor, and it should be gone by the next morning.

**483** **Deep clean concrete with soapy water.** Scrub really dusty, dirty concrete with soapy water and a scrub brush. Rinse carefully with the garden hose or buckets of clean water, and suck up excess water with a wet/dry vac. Leave the basement door open (if weather permits) and the dehumidifier running to air out the rest of the moisture left from cleaning.

**484** **Clean up efflorescence.** Efflorescence is a white powder that can accumulate on concrete in basements. It's actually salt that is left behind when concrete floors or walls seep and the water evaporates. Clean it up with a scrub brush, mop, or cleaning cloth and some soapy water. If it returns, you may need to waterproof your basement.

**485** **Look for mold.** Mold is usually black or gray, but it can also be orange, brown, green, or white. Musty smells also indicate moisture and mold and mildew growth.

**486** **Kill mold and mildew with vodka.** Spray surfaces liberally with vodka to kill fungal growth. Let them sit for 30 minutes to an hour, then scrub clean with soapy water. Spray the surface again lightly to serve as a barrier against future growth. You can also use hydrogen peroxide in place of vodka if you prefer.

**487** **Prevent molds from forming with a dehumidifier.** Most basements have too much moisture, so to prevent issues that moisture can cause, such as mold and mildew growth, it's important to keep a dehumidifier running at all times to absorb moisture from the air.

**488** **Store belongings in plastic containers.** Cardboard boxes are not the best choice for storing items. Moisture can cause the cardboard to break down fast, rendering it unusable, and these boxes offer no protection against mold and mildew growth and pest infestations. To protect your belongings, store them in sealable plastic bags or bins. Stack the containers to preserve space, and consolidate if you can.

**489** **Use your vacuum hose to suck up cobwebs and dust.** Unless you already clean your basement and attic regularly, you'll probably have to deal with a lot of dust. Instead of wiping surfaces clean with a cloth, first vacuum up dirt and debris, or use a broom to sweep up the mess. Use your vacuum's attachments to reach smaller spaces. If you see signs of rodent infestation, set up traps, or call an exterminator.

**490** **Purge your belongings.** Now would be a great time to go through everything to see if you can sell it or give it away. If it's in your attic or basement and not being used regularly, chances are you don't really need it. Of course, the exceptions are seasonal items like holiday decorations.

**491** **Keep your basement and attic cleaner longer.** Reduce the amount of dirt and dust that accumulates in your attic and basement by sealing cracks and holes that may allow dirt, dust mites, and other pests into your home. Check for leaks, and seal them immediately to keep mold and mildew from getting out of control.

# GARAGES

**492** **Get rid of the clutter.** Find a new home for everything you don't need. Have a yard sale, give things away, or donate them. When your storage space is overflowing, you need to ask yourself repeatedly: "Do I really need this?" Go through your belongings at least once or twice a year to see if you can get rid of anything else.

**493** **Air it out.** Leave the garage door open for a while to remove any offensive odors and help the floor dry faster. Direct a fan across the floor to help moisture evaporate even more quickly. Clean surfaces and neutralize with a 50/50 solution of white vinegar and water used as a cleaning spray. Set out dishes full of baking soda to freshen even more.

**494** **Dispose of dangerous items properly.** Most areas have laws governing how you can dispose of toxic chemicals; electronics like computers, air conditioners, and printers; and other hazardous materials. Check with your town's sanitation department to see how they dispose of such items.

**495** **Remove dirt, dust, and debris.** Work from top to bottom, cleaning the floor last. Use a broom to remove cobwebs and dust from the walls and corners. Sweep the floor thoroughly. Mop with ½ tablespoon of Sal Suds in 3 gallons of water, using a deck brush to scrub the floor thoroughly, then rinse clean with a garden hose. Squeegee the floor to remove excess water, or use a wet/dry vac. Let the floor dry completely before putting your things back in the garage.

**496** **Inspect your garage door regularly.** Malfunctioning garage doors, especially motorized doors, can cause serious injuries. Regularly inspect the door and motor to ensure they are in good working order, and immediately fix any problems as they arise. Wipe the door and hardware clean with a damp cloth, paying special attention to the tracks. Don't lubricate the tracks, since doing so may cause the door to shift and become unbalanced.

## Chemical-Free Ways to Remove Stains from Concrete

All sorts of difficult stains can crop up on concrete. Never use a metal brush to scrub concrete, as it can scratch the surface and cause permanent damage. Use these tips to keep your garage and driveway looking great.

**497 Use powdered laundry detergent to remove barbecue grease.** Sprinkle powdered laundry detergent on the stain. Add a little water to form a thick paste, and scrub the mixture into the stain. Let it sit at least 30 minutes, then rinse.

**498 Treat motor oil stains with dish soap.** Squirt liquid dish soap on the stain, and scrub with a stiff-bristle brush. Let it sit for 30 minutes, and use the hose to rinse the soap away.

**499 Clean rust stains from concrete with Kool-Aid.** Combine a packet of Kool-Aid Lemonade powder with a few drops of hot water to form a paste. Apply it on the stain, and let it sit for 10 minutes. Scrub with a firm-bristle brush, then rinse with clean water.

**500 Use boiling water to get rid of moss and algae stains.** Pour a pot of boiling water over the stain, scrub with a brush, and rinse well with a high-pressure garden hose.

**501 Remove mildew stains with a pressure washer.**
Buy or rent a pressure washer so you can clean mildew from concrete surfaces without using any chemicals. If this doesn't work, spray the stain liberally with white vinegar, and let it sit for at least 30 minutes. Scrub clean, and rinse with a garden hose. You can also use hydrogen peroxide or vodka to clean mold and mildew stains. Be careful when cleaning mold and mildew. Cleaning can release spores into the air, so it's a good idea to wear a protective face mask, gloves, and eye protection, especially when scrubbing and hosing off the stains.

**502 Scrub away leaf stains with dish soap.** Squirt a little natural dish soap or Sal Suds on the stain, and add a little water to make it foam. Scrub the stain with a brush, then rinse well with high pressure from the hose.

**503 Swap commercial salt deicers for baking soda.**
Commercial salt deicers can stain concrete. Remove ice without the chemicals and staining by sprinkling with baking soda instead. This works because baking soda is a type of salt, and it lowers the freezing point of treated surfaces.

**504 Round up water with a cheap DIY floor squeegee.** Put a piece of foam pipe insulation over the tines of a gardening rake to quickly sweep water to a drain or out the door.

505 **Soak up spills effortlessly with sawdust.** Pour sawdust on the spill. Let it sit for 30 minutes, then sweep it up. No dealing with sopping towels! This trick even works for oil spills.

506 **Clean out your garage fast with a leaf blower.** Instead of spending all that time sweeping the floor, blow out dirt and debris the quick and easy way with your leaf blower. Put on gloves, a dust mask, safety glasses, and ear protection, and blow your mess right out the door.

507 **Use vertical space for storage.** Garages often have loads of unused vertical space. Build a shelf close to the ceiling for storage bins and coolers, and hang bicycles, kayaks, lawn care equipment, and more to free up floor space.

508 **Clean safety glasses in the dishwasher.** Toss your safety glasses in the top shelf of the dishwasher to remove dirt and gunk.

**509** **Renew old paintbrushes with vinegar.** Soak messy nylon paintbrushes in white vinegar for 30 minutes to loosen paint and soften bristles. Wash with soap and water, using your fingers to remove any remaining paint, then rinse well, and air-dry.

**510** **Help your vacuum reach new heights with a PVC pipe.** Attach a 10-foot PVC pipe, available in the plumbing aisle at your local hardware store, to your vacuum's hose, and use it to clean higher than ever before without using a ladder or step stool.

**511** **Remove grease from hands with a homemade sugar scrub.** Mix granulated sugar with enough water to form a paste, and use it to scrub motor oil right off hands!

**512** **Zap oil stains with soda.** Pour soda over the stain, let it sit overnight, then rinse with the hose.

# 513 Clean up all sorts of sticky messes with homemade all-natural gunk remover.

This DIY gunk remover does an amazing job of cleaning paint and grease from your hands and surfaces, including concrete, tools, plastic, and more—and is completely safe to use!

½ cup baking soda

½ cup coconut oil

10 drops lemon essential oil

1. Mix the baking soda and coconut oil in a small bowl until well combined. (You can use another kind of vegetable oil, such as olive oil, instead if that's what you have on hand.) Add the essential oil, and stir well.

2. To use, apply a dab to remove stickers and labels, and let them sit for 20 minutes. Rinse in warm water, and scrub the label with your finger or a cloth. To clean your skin, put a small glob in your hand, and rub it into your stained skin. Use a toothbrush for extra scrubbing power, if needed, then rinse and dry.

# Natural Ways to Clean and Prevent Rust

Since garages often hold tools, bicycles, cars, and other metal objects, you may find yourself dealing with a rust problem at some point. Commercial rust cleaners are especially harsh and dangerous to your health and the environment. Learn how to remove rust naturally with these safe and easy methods.

## 514 Scrub away rust with steel wool. The best place to start cleaning rust is with good old elbow grease. See how much rust you can scrub away with steel wool, a wire brush, sandpaper, or even a balled-up piece of aluminum foil.

## 515 Get more cleaning power with baking soda. Make a paste by mixing baking soda with a little water, making sure the paste is thick enough to stick to the rusty surface. Apply the paste, let it sit for 30 minutes to an hour, then scrub with steel wool.

## 516 Prevent rust before it starts. The easiest way to fight rust is to prevent it in the first place. Whenever possible, store metal items indoors and away from moist areas like basements. Store garden tools in a bucket full of sand to keep them dry and rust-free. Prime and paint objects that may be exposed to wet conditions, such as bikes, lawn furniture, and outdoor fixtures, to prevent rust from forming again.

**517 Use cola as a rust remover.** Soft drinks contain phosphoric acid, which is another good rust dissolver. Soak items in soda for 24 hours, then scrub and rinse thoroughly. You may want to follow up with some natural dish soap to remove any stickiness left behind by the sugar content. If the item is larger and can't be soaked, saturate a sponge with soda, apply it to the item, and scrub. For chrome fixtures on motorcycles, bicycles, and cars, put some cola on a piece of aluminum foil crumpled into a ball, and use it to scrub away light rust.

**518 Make a scrub with lemon and salt.** Sprinkle kosher salt on the rust, and add lemon juice. Let the mixture sit for just a few minutes, then start scrubbing, adding more salt and lemon juice, if needed. Don't let it sit too long, though, since lemon is an even stronger acid than white vinegar and can damage the metal underneath with prolonged contact. If you're using fresh lemon, cut the lemon in half and use the salt and lemon like a scrub sponge. Just like with vinegar, you'll want to make sure to rinse well after cleaning.

**519 Mix lemon and vinegar for a superstrong cleaner.** Soak rusty items in a solution with a 1:1 ratio of white vinegar and lemon juice for the strongest cleaning yet! You'll want to keep an eye on this cleaning method, however, since this soaking mixture is even stronger than using vinegar or lemon alone. Please note that the acids in vinegar and lemon juice may temporarily turn items black, but this should go away after rinsing with water.

**520** **Clean tough rust buildup with vinegar.** The acetic acid content in vinegar dissolves rust, so if you're not making much headway with scrubbing, try soaking rusty objects in white vinegar. Just be sure to rinse objects thoroughly after cleaning since prolonged exposure may cause permanent damage.

**521** **For really stubborn rust, use diluted ammonia.** If none of these natural hacks are working, you may need to resort to something even stronger. Some people use ammonia in natural cleaning, but it's actually pretty toxic. Just be careful when handling, always wear gloves and eye protection, and keep out of reach of children and pets. To remove rust, mix 1 teaspoon of ammonia for every cup of warm water, and soak the items. Check at least once per hour, and scrub away any loosened rust. Once the rust is removed, be sure to clean the item with soapy water, and rinse thoroughly to ensure no ammonia is left behind.

**522** **Remove light rust with a potato.** Potatoes naturally contain oxalic acid, which dissolves rust. Cut a raw potato in half, sprinkle some kosher salt on the area, and use the potato to scrub the rust away.

# CAR CLEANING HACKS

The all-natural cleaning craze has yet to reach car maintenance on a commercial level, but you can get ahead of the curve with these easy and effective DIY tips and recipes that'll help save the environment and your wallet.

523 **Vacuum before you dust.** In the house, you typically dust first, then vacuum, but the car is different. Since it's such a small, cramped space, you'll get the job done faster if you remove all the dry dirt and hair from the dash, seats, and floors first. That way, you can just suck up the dirt quickly instead of struggling to clean it up with a cloth.

524 **Clean hard-to-reach areas with various things you already have around the house.** Clean, dry paint or makeup brushes pull double duty to remove dust from air vents. A small, damp painting sponge, cotton balls, and cotton swabs work great on stubborn dirt. If these areas are really dusty, follow along with a vacuum to catch the dirt and dust right away as you clean.

**525 Start cleaning at the top to work more efficiently.** Work from top to bottom so you won't have to clean a surface more than once.

**526 Brush the carpet to loosen dirt the vacuum may leave behind.** Use a stiff brush to loosen dirt before vacuuming. Even large industrial vacuums can have a difficult time picking up dirt embedded in those tight carpet fibers.

**527 Keep the car tidy with a plastic cereal container.** Use a plastic cereal container as a trash can to keep your car clean, then empty it when you reach a gas station or get home. This tip is especially helpful for long drives.

**528 Protect your cup holders with cupcake liners.** Cleaning stuck-on messes in your cup holders can be difficult and time consuming. Prevent the mess by lining them with silicone cupcake liners that are much easier to remove and clean.

# 529 Keep reusable wipes on hand to clean messes instantly.

Citrus essential oils clean and condition car surfaces, and the all-natural cleaning solution is mild and safe enough to clean hands. These wipes are essential for car trips!

1½ cups water

½ cup vodka

3 tablespoons liquid Castile soap or Sal Suds

30 drops lemon essential oil

30 drops orange oil

Washcloths or other soft fabric squares

1-quart glass Mason jar (widemouthed jars work best for easy access)

1. Mix the ingredients in a Mason jar or other glass container with a lid. Screw the lid on tight, and shake well to combine.
2. Add as many washcloths as you can fit into the container. You should be able to fit at least 6 regular-sized washcloths. Old cut-up towels and T-shirts also work well. Replace the lid, and shake again to wet the cloths.
3. To use, remove a cloth, wring out the excess cleaning liquid back into the container, and wipe surfaces clean. When the washcloths get dirty, launder with other cleaning towels, and reuse.

**530 Prevent stains on upholstery with seat covers.**
Do you have pets or kids, or just a messy partner? Protect your car's upholstery—and its resale value—by using washable seat covers.

**531 Clean your windows last.** Since dirty windows can be a safety hazard, it's even more important to get car windows as clean as possible. Leave the windows for last to ensure they don't get marked up while you wipe down other surfaces.

**532 Don't forget the top edges of windows.** Roll down your windows just a little bit to reveal the dirt around the top edges. Wipe clean.

**533 Shine your car lights with vodka and pantyhose.** Keeping your headlights clean and polished will help you see and make you more visible to other drivers. Spray your lights with vodka, then buff clean with pantyhose.

**534** **Use a DIY spray for streak-free windows.** With all the grease and grime from the road, your car's windows may need some extra cleaning power, and this easy homemade spray cleaner is sure to do the trick! Mix 1 cup of water, 1 cup of vodka, and 2 tablespoons of white vinegar in a spray bottle, and shake to combine. Spray windows inside and out, then wipe clean with a microfiber cloth.

**535** **Clean your headlights with toothpaste.** Put a dab of plain white toothpaste on a cloth, rub it on your headlights, then wipe clean to make them crystal clear.

**536** **Remove light upholstery stains with baking soda.** Make a paste with 3 tablespoons of baking soda and 1 tablespoon of water, and apply it to your car's upholstery. Scrub to remove dirt and stains, let it air-dry, then vacuum up the residue. This method will neutralize funky odors too!

# 537 Nix tough stains with a DIY maximum-strength upholstery cleaner.

If your upholstery is badly stained, white vinegar and baking soda may not be enough to get it all out. This recipe brings out the toughest options—borax and Castile soap—to get out the most stubborn stains in no time!

2 cups boiling water

2 tablespoons borax

3 tablespoons grated soap (I like to use Castile soap)

8–10 drops essential oil (optional—try pine essential oil for a traditional car smell or peppermint to improve alertness and mental clarity)

Scrub brush

1. Mix all of the ingredients in a bowl, and stir gently until the soap dissolves. Add 8–10 drops of your favorite essential oils, if desired, to make your car smell nice.

2. Take a stiff scrub brush, dip it in your cleaner, and scrub messes out of seats, floor mats, and carpeting. Wipe clean with a damp cloth, dipping the cloth in a bucket of clean water, as needed. Allow upholstery to air-dry completely.

**538** **Rinse your car before washing to prevent scratches.** If you start washing your car without rinsing it first, you'll just grind in the dirt that's on the surface of the car, and you may ruin your paint finish.

**539** **Use two buckets to get your car really clean.** Use one bucket for soapy water and the other for clean rinse water. After you scrub your car with a microfiber mitt or cloth, dunk it in the rinse water before grabbing the suds again so you won't fill your soapy water with grease and grime.

**540** **Shine up your dash with olive oil.** Use a dab of olive oil to polish your car's vinyl and leather surfaces and keep them from cracking.

# 541 Save money and the environment with DIY all-natural car wash concentrate.

¼ cup dish soap

¼ cup baking soda

Water

1-gallon jug with a twist-top lid

1. Add the dish soap and baking soda, then fill the jug the rest of the way with water. Shake to combine.
2. To use, shake again to mix, and add 1 cup per 2 gallons of warm water. Clean your car's exterior with the solution and a microfiber mitt or cloth.

# 542 Wash your car when it's cool to prevent streaks.
When you wash your car's exterior when it's warm from driving or sitting in direct sunlight, you may be left with a splotchy, streaked finish. To combat this, try to wash your car after it's cooled from driving or when the sun isn't so high in the sky.

## 543 Ditch the sponge to prevent scratches.
Sponges can hold on to dirt as they clean, and all that embedded dirt can scratch your car. Use a microfiber mitt or cloth to clean instead. Unlike sponges, microfiber lets dirt fall away easily every time you rinse.

## 544 Make a gentle scrub sponge with pantyhose.
Put your sponge in a pair of pantyhose to scrub your car without scratching.

## 545 Wax your car a couple times a year to keep it cleaner longer.
When a car is protected with wax, dust and dirt lift away easily. Plus, it helps protect the paint job.

## 546 Dry your car after washing to prevent water marks.
Leaving your car to air-dry after washing or driving around when the car is still wet can cause water marks and streaks to form. To prevent this, dry your car with a microfiber towel or other absorbent, soft cloth, being careful not to pick up any dirt that may scratch your car's paint.

## 547 Use baking soda and essential oils for an easy DIY air freshener.

½ cup baking soda

8–10 drops essential oil

1-pint Mason jar

1. Stir the ingredients to combine. Poke 4–5 small holes in the lid with a nail, and pop the jar in a cup holder to keep your car smelling fresh and clean.
2. Replace the mixture every month.

## 548 Buff wax with a microfiber towel. Wipe the wax in a circular motion, and refold the cloth as you wipe, so you're always using a fresh, clean cloth. Replace the cloth once the first one is covered in wax.

## 549 Wash your car's exterior with hair conditioner for a freshly waxed look. Get that clean, waxed look without all the work of applying car wax by washing your car with hair conditioner that contains lanolin.

550 **Remove tough back-road messes with cream of tartar.** Cut through greasy, grimy windshield messes from driving on back roads by sprinkling your windshield with cream of tartar. Scrub the windshield with soapy water, and rinse thoroughly.

551 **Clean your windshield in a pinch with feminine hygiene products.** Did you run out of windshield washer fluid and just happen to have some sanitary napkins on hand? Rub your windshield vigorously with the pad to get it nice and clean until you can replace the washer fluid.

552 **Remove tar and sap from your car with mayonnaise.** Cover the stain with mayo, and let it sit for 30 minutes. Wipe clean with a cloth or paper towel.

553 **Use a squeegee to clean pet hair from upholstery.** Spray pet hair lightly with plain water or natural cleaning spray if that's what you have on hand, then wipe it up with a squeegee.

**554** **Clean stuck-on bugs with baking soda.** Make a paste with baking soda and water, and apply it to your car's grille. Let it sit for 10 minutes, then scrub with a moist sponge.

**555** **Eliminate stickers with ease.** Use a plastic putty knife to scrape off stickers without scratching. Clean up any sticky residue with the DIY gunk remover mentioned earlier in this chapter.

**556** **Deep clean your windshield wipers to prevent streaks.** When your wipers are dirty, they'll streak the glass instead of cleaning. Lift the wipers away from the windshield, and spray them with a 50/50 mixture of white vinegar and water. Wipe clean with a cloth or paper towels, and lower them into place.

**557** **Prevent your car's paint from rusting with clear nail polish.** Coat small scratches, dents, and wear in your car's paint with clear nail polish to keep these weak spots from spreading and rusting.

**558** **Melt ice instantly with homemade deicer spray.** Mix 1 cup of water and 1 cup of vodka in a spray bottle, and shake to combine. Spray windshields and locks to melt ice quickly and naturally.

**559** **Stop a crack in your windshield with clear nail polish.** Move your car into the shade, and paint the crack with clear nail polish on both sides of the glass. You will still need to replace the windshield, but this trick should buy you some time.

**560** **Make your own inexpensive and effective natural windshield washer fluid.** Mix 4 cups of water, 3 cups of vodka, and 2 teaspoons of natural dish soap in a 1-gallon jug with a screw-top lid. Shake to combine, then add to the washer fluid reservoir.

# 8. EVERYTHING ELSE

In this chapter, we'll cover miscellaneous items not covered in other chapters, lay out some "house rules" to make cleaning easier, and design a cleaning schedule that will help you make sure your spaces stay tidy so you can avoid marathon cleaning sessions.

# House Rules

These simple hacks can stop messes from accumulating in your house in the first place.

**561** **Leave your shoes at the door.** Make a rule to never wear outdoor shoes inside. If you want to take it to the next level, offer guests a pair of slippers to use, or let them know beforehand so that they can bring their own. If you have dogs, keep a towel at the door to wipe their paws before they come in. The less dirt and debris you track into your house, the less you'll have to clean up!

**562** **Clean messes right away.** It may be tempting to leave spills, clutter, and other messes for later, but you'll be better off in the long run if you take a few minutes to clean them up right away. Spills can be harder to clean after they've dried up, and if you keep leaving messes for later, those chores will quickly add up and overwhelm you.

**563** **Give everything a place.** Reduce clutter by giving all your belongings a designated (hidden, if possible) space, then put them away when you're not actively using them. For example, do you only use the mixer and all its attachments once a month? Put it in a cabinet for the rest of the time. Have random chargers strewn all over the house? Set up a central charging station for everyone's electronics. That way, all the chargers have a home, and everyone knows where to find them.

**564 Keep dirty clothes in laundry baskets.** Your house will be a lot cleaner if you don't have piles of clothes lying around everywhere. Plus, when you go to do the laundry, all the clothes will be in one place and ready to go.

**565 Never go empty-handed.** If you're heading upstairs, take something with you that needs to be put away up there, and vice versa. That way, you won't have to make extra trips to clear up clutter.

**566 Pick up the kitchen after every meal.** Do the dishes and wipe the counter and stovetop after every meal or at least every night. It's so much nicer to wake up to a clean kitchen, and you won't have to worry about odors and bacteria forming on dirty dishes.

**567 Clean floors more than once a week.** Take 5 or 10 minutes to sweep or vacuum high-traffic areas at the end of the day. That way, your floor will always look nice and clean.

**568 Brush the dog.** Even if your dog's fur doesn't tangle easily, she still probably sheds and leaves a mess in your home. Reduce hair "tumbleweeds" by taking your dog outside to brush away dead hair either every day or every other day, depending on how much she sheds. Then leave her hair outside to be used by birds and other wildlife.

**569 Change your schedule, as needed.** Your cleaning schedule and even some of these house rules aren't set in stone. Feel free to change them as often as you need to so that they fit in your lifestyle.

**570 Store your cleaning supplies where you use them.** Keep your bathroom cleaners in your bathroom, kitchen cleaners in the kitchen—you get the idea. That way, you don't have to lug your cleaning supplies all over the house, because they are already right where you need them.

**571 Clean more often.** The key to cleaning faster is to clean more often. Have you ever noticed that cleaning your home takes much longer after you've skipped a week or two? It's actually much easier in the long run to clean as you go instead of putting it off until later. Tidy up every night, do the dishes and wipe counters after every meal, and clean up messes right away. With this method, you can clean in short bursts instead of spending hours cleaning bigger messes, and when someone drops in unexpectedly, your home won't be a complete disaster.

## 30-Minute Speed-Cleaning Plan

Did you just find out you're getting some unexpected guests, or do you have a particularly full schedule this week? Use these speed-cleaning tricks when you just don't have enough time to clean.

**572** **Lose the clutter.** Do you have tons of newspapers, magazines, kids' homework, and other clutter lying around? Do a clean sweep, and tidy it up. Put it into neat stacks, or throw it all in a plastic bin or drawer to sort out later.

**573** **Wash the dishes and wipe down kitchen counters.** Use burner covers to hide stovetop messes.

**574** **Empty the trash can.** If your trash is overflowing, your guests are bound to notice, and it takes only a minute anyway.

**575** **Vacuum main areas only.** Do a quick cleaning of the floors only where you and your guests will be visiting.

**576** **Quick-clean the bathroom.** No one wants to use a dirty bathroom. Wipe down the mirror, sink, and toilet. Close the shower curtain, and clean the bathtub another day. If the toilet isn't very dirty, just give it a once-over with the toilet brush. If the toilet needs a little more attention, use some toilet cleaner.

# HALLWAYS AND STAIRCASES

Hallways and staircases tend to be high-traffic areas, so they can get pretty dirty. However, since they're only used to get from point A to point B inside your home, they're often forgotten when cleaning.

**577** **Mop wood stairs with floor cleaner.** Add 1½ teaspoons of Sal Suds to 1 gallon of water, and use a mop or microfiber cloth to wipe stairs clean.

**578** **Don't forget doorframes.** Doorframes collect tons of dust, but they're so high up that you may not notice how dirty they can get. Use a feather duster or dry cloth to clean lightly soiled doorframes, or a damp microfiber cloth for tougher messes.

**579** **Disinfect handrails with hydrogen peroxide.** Give railings a spritz of hydrogen peroxide or vodka before wiping clean to kill germs that can make you and your family sick.

# 580 Vacuum the upstairs hallway last.

Clean the floor in the upstairs hallway after you clean all the bedrooms. Work backward toward the staircase, then down the stairs.

# 581 Wipe down the walls, along with dust moldings and baseboards.

Wipe down the walls with a cloth dipped in soapy water, or use a microfiber mop to avoid bending and reaching. Don't neglect the dust that collects on baseboards and moldings. Wipe them down with a damp cloth.

# 582 Use a damp cloth to clean bannisters and other woodwork.

After cleaning these areas with a damp cloth, follow up with a dry cloth to avoid streaks.

## Simple Ways to Get Motivated to Clean

With the stress of our busy lifestyles, jobs, and family responsibilities, even simple daily household chores can get overwhelming. Learn how to motivate yourself to clean even when the mess feels overpowering.

583 **Start small.** If you have a whole house to clean, you might shut down thinking of how much you have to do: clean the kitchen, tidy clutter in the living room, change the bedding, start the laundry. Just focus on one thing at a time. Pick one thing to do, get it done, then move on to something else. You'll see how great it looks when you're done and have renewed motivation to keep going.

584 **Rock out.** Listen to your favorite music while you work. Make sure it's upbeat to give you energy to get things done.

585 **Picture it clean.** Think of how great your house will look and how accomplished you'll feel when your chores are all done. If you need more visual motivation, take pictures of your house when it's clean to remind you of how awesome your house can look.

586 **Clean in the morning.** Wake up, start the coffee, and get going! The sun is shining, and you're all ready to seize the day. If you can't bear the thought of a full day of cleaning, really give it your all until lunchtime, then go do something fun.

**587** **Set a schedule—and stick to it.** Make your cleaning schedule nonnegotiable. Pretty soon, it will be routine and won't feel like such a huge chore.

**588** **Avoid distractions.** You can easily waste an hour or two scrolling through your phone. Skip the distractions, focus on cleaning, and you'll be done before you know it.

**589** **Clean through the week.** Spread out your chores though the week. Do a little every night, then take the weekend off from your to-do list. You'll always have something to look forward to and designated free time.

**590** **Reward yourself.** Be sure to reward yourself for a job well done! Set a goal like sticking to your cleaning schedule for a month or washing the dishes every night for a week. Once you reach your goal, give yourself incentive to keep going. Get that new yoga mat or outfit you've been wanting, or go out to dinner with friends. You deserve it!

**591** **Don't beat yourself up.** Even if you don't get as much done as you'd like, don't be too hard on yourself. You'll only make yourself more stressed out about cleaning.

**592** **Ask for help.** If you live with other people, you shouldn't have to do all the work—don't be afraid to ask your family or roommates to help out. Giving kids chores can help prepare them for adulthood, and you can get the job done much quicker and go do something fun if you all pitch in!

# CLOSETS

Closets are often the dumping ground for miscellaneous items, which can leave them bursting at the seams. Learn how to purge unwanted belongings, tidy up, and deep clean your closets with these easy tips!

594 **Empty your closet.** Take everything out. You need to inventory what's there and organize from scratch.

594 **Deep clean your closet.** If it's lightly soiled, just give it a once-over with a damp cloth and some cleaning spray. If you haven't cleaned it in years, you might want to get a bucket of soapy water and really wipe it down. Clean everything—the walls, shelves, moldings, baseboards, and doorframes. Vacuum or sweep the floor, and mop bare floors.

595 **Air it out.** The next step is to sort through your belongings, so while you're doing that, air out your closet to get rid of any stale smells. Spray some DIY room freshener throughout the closet, and let it work its magic.

**596** **Sort through your stuff.** Put items into four piles: what to keep, what you can do without (the "maybe" pile), what to throw away, and what you can donate. Try to repurpose clothing in the trash pile as cleaning rags. Look at your "maybe" pile again. Try on clothes to be sure they fit, and donate anything you can stand to live without. Remember, you're trying to lose the clutter here!

**597** **Put everything back in the closet.** Make everything neat and tidy. Make sure you have enough hangers for all your clothes and jackets. Put off-season clothes and other rarely used items in storage bins with tight lids to keep them dirt- and dust-free.

**598** **Make a DIY no-slip hanger with pipe cleaners.** Wrap pipe cleaners around clothes hangers where the shoulder of the garment rests on the hanger to keep clothes from slipping.

## How Often Should You Clean Common Items?

### Every Day

O Make the bed.

O Spray shower with DIY shower spray.

O Wash dishes.

O Wipe counters and stovetop.

O Sweep and vacuum floors in high-traffic spots.

O Do laundry as needed.

O Tidy up clutter and clean messes.

### Every Week

O Change bedding.

O Vacuum and mop floors.

O Vacuum upholstery.

O Scour and dust.

O Clean the microwave.

O Wipe down kitchen appliances.

O Sanitize sponges, and replace every 3–4 weeks.

O Rinse drains with hot or boiling water.

O Clean and sanitize makeup brushes.

O Wipe off electronics.

### Every Month

O Dust light fixtures.

O Clean heating and cooling vents.

O Deep clean grout.

O Clean windows and blinds.

O Wipe down inside of refrigerator.

O Clean the oven and dishwasher.

- ○ Deep clean coffee maker.
- ○ Wash trash cans.
- ○ Clean the washer and dryer.
- ○ Launder throw rugs.
- ○ Wash pillow covers.
- ○ Dust baseboards and moldings.
- ○ Clean and disinfect humidifiers.
- ○ Clean ceiling fans.
- ○ Wipe pantry shelves and inside cabinets.
- ○ Discard expired food.

## Every 3–6 Months

- ○ Launder washable curtains. (Note: washing curtains can reduce their life span. Only launder curtains when they are visibly soiled.)
- ○ Clean comforters.
- ○ Vacuum, rotate, and deep clean the mattress.
- ○ Launder washable slipcovers.
- ○ Wash shower curtain liner.
- ○ Clean your vacuum.
- ○ Deep clean the freezer.
- ○ Clean books. Wipe books clean, and flip through the pages to prevent discoloration.

## Every Year

- ○ Wash pillows (1–2 times per year, as needed).
- ○ Clean the fireplace, and hire a chimney sweep.
- ○ Clear the gutters.
- ○ Clean dryer vents.
- ○ Shampoo carpets.

**599 Clean your windows on overcast days to prevent streaks.** Washing your windows on warm, sunny days can cause your cleaning spray to evaporate too quickly and leave a streaky mess. Try to clean windows outside of peak daylight hours or on overcast days.

**600 Prevent frost on windows with salt water.** Dip a cloth in salt water, and use it to wipe the outside of your windows. Try this trick on car windows too!

**601 Dust blinds with kitchen tongs.** Grab a pair of tongs, 2 microfiber cloths, and 4 rubber bands. Wrap a cloth around each tong, and secure each cloth with 2 rubber bands. Once the cloths are attached to the tongs, grasp each blind between the 2 microfiber cloths, and wipe along the length of the blind. You can also spray the cloths or blinds with all-purpose spray to help loosen dirt and dust.

## 602 Get a streak-free shine with cornstarch.

Amazingly, cornstarch works wonders to make windows shiny and crystal clear.

1 cup white vinegar

1 cup water

1 teaspoon cornstarch

5–10 drops essential oil

Spray bottle

1. Place all the ingredients in a spray bottle, and shake to combine. Shake well before each use.
2. Spray glass and mirrors, wipe clean with a clean microfiber cloth, then buff with a polishing cloth for a streak-free shine.

## 603 Use a sock to clean window blinds. Make use of unpaired socks from the laundry! Put a sock on your hand, and dampen with water or all-purpose spray. Grab each blind between your thumb and fingers, and wipe clean.

**604** **Wash the outside of your windows with a homemade window cleaner.** Mix 1 cup of white vinegar, 8 cups of water, and 2 teaspoons of natural dish soap in a bucket. Rinse the windows with the garden hose. Use a mop to scrub the windows with the solution, then rinse clean. Follow up with a squeegee to eliminate streaks.

**605** **Shake curtains clean instead of washing.** Laundering curtains can reduce their life span, and some curtains are too delicate to be washed at all. To clean curtains without damaging them, shake them to loosen dirt and debris, then vacuum any remaining dust with the upholstery attachment.

**606** **Steam clean heavy curtains.** Heavier curtains don't usually clean up well in the washing machine. Since they're so heavy, they hold on to moisture, making them even more difficult to dry completely and prone to mold and mildew. Instead, try steam cleaning. You don't even need to take your curtains off the rods! Just make sure not to get your curtains too wet when steam cleaning so they won't take too long to dry. You may want to clean them on a sunny day to help them dry more quickly.

**607 Clean dirt and pet hair from window screens with a lint roller.** Run a lint roller across the surface of your window screens to remove pet hair, dirt, cobwebs, and other debris effortlessly.

**608 Mend a torn window screen with clear nail polish.** Fix little snags in your window screens with a coat of nail polish to keep them from getting bigger.

**609 Remove dirt from window tracks with a toilet paper roll.** If your vacuum's crevice attachment isn't small enough to fit in window tracks, take the cardboard tube from the center of your toilet paper roll, and attach to the end of the vacuum hose. Bend the tube flat to fit in the track, and use it to clean those hard-to-reach places.

**610 Scrub away stuck-on dirt from window tracks with a toothbrush.** Sprinkle some baking soda on greasy, grimy window tracks, then pour some white vinegar to make them bubble and fizz. Use a toothbrush to reach into the tracks and scrub dirt away, then wipe clean with a cloth or paper towels.

# CLEANING SUPPLIES

It may seem strange to clean your cleaning supplies, but doing so will help them work better and last longer. Always be sure to turn off and unplug electronic tools before cleaning.

## 611 Launder cleaning towels and cloths alone.
Even if you have just a few cleaning rags, it's still a good idea to put them in the wash for their own cycle. Sure, they're getting clean, but you still don't want dirt and grease to transfer to your bath towels or terry cloth lint to get on your microfiber towels.

## 612 Clean sponges with a salt soak or in the microwave.
Fill a bowl with cold water, add 3 table-spoons of salt, and stir to dissolve. Add the sponge, and let it soak overnight. You can also microwave wet sponges for 2 minutes to kill germs. Replace disposable sponges every 3–4 weeks, or sooner if they become really soiled. For a more environmentally friendly option, buy sponges that are machine washable, and just toss them in the washing machine every 1–2 weeks.

## Quick and Easy Steps to a Clean Vacuum Cleaner

You might think of a vacuum only when you need to clean other things, but it needs maintenance too. These simple tips will keep yours running well.

**613** **Empty dirt and debris regularly to keep your vacuum flowing freely.** Empty the canister on your bagless vacuum after every use or when it's about halfway full, and replace bags when ½ to ⅔ full. This may seem like a waste, but since vacuums run more easily when they're not completely full, replacing bags more often can actually help the vacuums last longer.

**614** **Clean the attachments.** Take off removable attachments, and wash them in warm, soapy water, rinse thoroughly, and dry completely. Never get attachments and other parts wet if they contain any wires or are permanently attached to the machine.

**615** **Increase suction by removing blockages.** Most cases of reduced suction are caused by blockages. To remove a clog, turn off and unplug the machine. Check the vacuum brushes, hose, and hose entrance for dirt and debris, and remove what you can reach. If you can't remove a blockage inside the hose, detach the hose from the machine, and soak it in warm, soapy water to help loosen the clog.

**616 Remove and clean filters to keep dust and allergens away.** Vacuums have filters to remove dust and allergens from the air. Consult your user manual to see if the filters in your vacuum are washable. If they are, remove the filters, and tap them against a trash can to remove loose dirt and debris. Wash in warm water, and dry overnight to ensure they're completely dry before putting them back in the machine. If the filters are not washable, simply remove the filters and tap against the trash can to remove dirt, gently rub away the rest of the dirt with a cloth or paper towels, and replace in the machine. HEPA filters usually cannot be washed and should be replaced about 2 times per year.

**617 Quickly remove obstructions from brush heads.** The brush heads on upright vacuums rotate to clean dirt from carpets. Regularly check brush heads to make sure they are free from any obstructions, such as hair, strings, and carpet fibers. If the brush heads are clogged, cut away fibers instead of pulling them out, being careful not to cut the brushes.

**618 Clean under the bottom plate.** If the brush heads seem especially clogged and dirty, remove the bottom plate and brush roll to clean underneath. The bottom plate will attach to the machine with latches or screws, and the brush roll should slide right out. Brush away debris with a scrub brush or dry cloth, and put the vacuum back together.

# 619 Deep clean the canister in soapy water.

Remove the canister from your bagless vacuum, and wipe the inside of the canister with a microfiber cloth. Wash the canister in warm, soapy water, rinse thoroughly, and dry completely before returning to the vacuum.

# 620 Wipe down the outside of the vacuum.

Your vacuum won't get your home very clean if it's covered in dirt and pet hair! Remember to wipe it down regularly or when it's looking messy with a lightly damp microfiber cloth. When wiping the cord, be sure to check it for any nicks and cuts, and fix any problems immediately to prevent any electrical issues.

# 621 Degrease your vacuum with cleaning spray.

If your vacuum seems extra soiled or even greasy, spray the outside lightly with vodka or natural all-purpose cleaning spray, and wipe with a clean, dry cloth. This will also help disinfect the machine and keep your home cleaner.

# 622 Remove scuff marks with vodka.

Scuff marks may form on your vacuum when you hit it against furniture and other obstacles when cleaning. Spray a little vodka on these marks, and buff them away with a dry cloth.

**623** **Disinfect your toilet brush.** Think of all the germs that must be on that little brush! Fill the brush holder with vinegar or vodka to kill bacteria between uses, and replace the brush about every 6 months.

**624** **Clean your broom in soapy water.** When you notice your broom is dingier than your dirty floors, it's time to clean it up. Soak it in a bucket of warm water and dish soap. Help release the dirt and grime by running your hands lightly back and forth across the bristles. Rinse with clean water, and let it air-dry before storing. You should also spray your broom with disinfectant after every use.

**625** **Throw your mopheads in the washing machine.** After every use or so, clean your mopheads, steam cleaner pads, and microfiber mopping cloths. Don't use commercial fabric softener, because it can reduce their ability to absorb water and make them useless for cleaning.

# 626 Deep clean feather dusters in soapy water.

Most of the time, you can clean your feather duster by taking it outside and shaking out the dirt and dust, but once a month or so, you'll want to deep clean it to ensure it can do its job. Fill a sink with warm, soapy water, and submerge the feather duster. Very gently swish it around to remove dirt and oils, then lightly squeeze out excess water. Don't wring the duster, or feathers may come out. Hang it to dry.

# 627 Hang up your mops and brooms.

Store your mops, brooms, and dustpans hanging up to save room on storage, help mops dry more efficiently, and prevent brooms from bending.

## Nifty Ways to Clean Up after Your Pet

Keeping pets in your home has many benefits, including reduced stress, improved immunity, and increased activity levels, but animals also come with their own set of cleaning challenges. Learn how to clean up after your pet with these quick and easy tips.

**628** **DIY a covered litter box with a storage bin.** Cut a hole in the side of a plastic storage bin, making sure the hole is large enough for your kitty to get in and out of the box, then add some kitty litter. Your cat will enjoy the privacy, and your home will smell much better with a covered box.

**629** **Keep pets off the furniture with plastic carpet protectors.** Put carpet protectors with the prickly side up on chairs, couches, and other furniture to train pets to stay away.

**630** **Remove nasty skunk odors with baking soda, dish soap, and hydrogen peroxide.** If you or your pet were unfortunate enough to meet with a skunk, try this all-natural anti-skunk remedy. Mix ½ cup of baking soda, 1 tablespoon of natural dish soap, and 1 quart of hydrogen peroxide in a bucket. Use the mixture to wash away the offensive odor, making sure to keep it away from sensitive areas like your eyes, nose, and mouth. Once the odor is removed, rinse thoroughly.

**631** **Store pet food in an airtight plastic container.**
Keep their food fresh and safe from pests by transferring to a plastic container.

**632** **Catch food and water with a waterproof dining placemat.** Put a place mat under your pet's food dishes to prevent food messes on your floor.

**633** **Protect a pet's paws and your floors with a foot soak.** Ice melt isn't just hard on a pet's paws; it can also damage your floors. Put a bucket of warm water and a towel at the door before you head out for your walk. When you get back, use the water to rinse their paws, then rub them dry with the towel.

**634** **Let vomit dry on carpets, then clean.** The rule of thumb with most stains is to treat them as soon as possible, but pet vomit is the one exception to this rule. It's actually easier to clean off carpeting if you let it dry first, then you can just vacuum it up. If a stain is left behind, just blot it with some plain (unflavored) club soda.

**635** **Stop dogs from digging with citrus peels.** (Most dogs dislike the scent of citrus.) Scatter orange, lemon, or grapefruit peels where you don't want your dog to dig up your yard. This will keep your yard looking pristine and your dog's paws nice and clean.

# CLEANING OUTSIDE

**636** **Remove dirt and grime from your siding with a pressure washer.** Buy or rent a pressure washer, and use it to remove dirt, grease, and mildew growth from your home's siding without scrubbing. Lay tarps or other heavy plastic over plants to protect them from damage. While you're at it, clean the porches, patio, and deck too.

**637** **Use a pressure washer to clean patio cushions without scrubbing.** Remove dirt and stains easily from your patio cushions by spraying with a pressure washer. Be sure to test whether the fabric can withstand the pressure before cleaning the entire cushion.

**638** **Clean outdoor rugs with baking soda and water pressure.** Rinse dirt and debris from the rug, then sprinkle liberally with baking soda. Work the baking soda into the rug with a deck brush, and scrub away dirt and stains. Let the baking soda sit for 10–15 minutes, then spray clean with a hose. Allow to air-dry in the sun.

**639** **Use Sal Suds to clean outdoor toys.** Rinse toys with the hose. Put ½ tablespoon of Sal Suds in a bucket, and add about 3 gallons of water. You can also use liquid Castile soap or natural dish soap if you prefer. Dip a microfiber car cleaning mitt, and use it to scrub dirt and grime from the toys. Rinse clean, and air-dry. The microfiber mitt makes this process a bit easier, but you can also just use a cloth or sponge.

**640** **Wash your cooler after every use.** If you clean your cooler every time you use it, you'll never need to deep clean it! Simply rinse with the garden hose, and allow to air-dry completely before storing.

**641** **Deep clean your cooler with baking soda and vinegar.** Mix ¼ cup of baking soda and enough water to form a paste. Apply the paste to any stains inside the cooler, and let them sit for 15 minutes. Use the rest of the paste and a bottle brush or sponge to scrub the cooler inside and out. Pour some white vinegar into the cooler to dissolve the baking soda and deodorize the cooler. Rinse with the garden hose, and allow to air-dry in the sun before storing.

**642** **Clean your flowerpots to keep your plants healthy.** Use a brush to remove dirt and debris. Fill a sink with warm water, and add natural dish soap and 1 cup of white vinegar. Hand-wash the pots just as you would your dishes, rinse well, and air-dry. If you don't want to wash them in your sink, use a storage bin or bucket, and clean them outside with the hose.

**643** **Spray your latex paint roller clean with the hose.** To make cleanup a breeze, hold your paint roller in a 5-gallon bucket, and hose it down clean with the garden hose. Use the hose to spin the paint roller to remove paint in a flash, then wash with soap, rinse, and dry.

# Unusual Cleaning Hacks

These tips and tricks are seriously unusual, but they actually work!

**644** **Remove gum from hair with cola.** If you get gum stuck in your hair, there's no need to cut it out. Just pour some cola in a small bowl, and soak the gum for a couple minutes until it loosens from the strands.

**645** **Defog goggles with toothpaste.** Put a dab of plain white toothpaste on a cloth, and rub it on the inside surface of the goggles to keep them from fogging up when you're swimming.

**646** **Clean eyeglasses with vodka.** Spritz eyeglass lenses with a little vodka, and wipe with a polishing cloth to make them crystal clear.

**647** **Use toothpaste to repair a scratched CD.** Wash the CD with a damp microfiber cloth. When cleaning CDs, always wipe in a circular motion from the middle to the outer edge. Put a dab of baking soda toothpaste (you want to use a gritty toothpaste, not a gel) on a lint-free cloth. Use it to rub the toothpaste into the scratch and buff it away, then rinse the CD. Dry gently.

**648** **Whiten piano keys with toothpaste.** Put a dab of plain white toothpaste on a cloth, and use it to wipe piano keys clean.

**649** **Store your paintbrush in the freezer between coats.** After you apply your first coat, put the paintbrush in a plastic bag, and store it in the freezer. The paint won't dry, so you can take it out and use it for the next coat. This way, you'll need to wash the paintbrush only when the job's finished!

**650** **Stay organized by assigning different colors to your kids.** Assign a color to each kid, then buy towels, cups, toothbrushes, and more for them to use exclusively. They'll always know which one is theirs, and it'll make sorting so much easier for you.

**651** **Pick up hard-to-reach coins and other small objects with your vacuum and a pair of pantyhose.** Put the foot of a pair of pantyhose over your vacuum's hose attachment, and use it to pick up coins without sucking them into the machine.

**652** **Fill nail holes in walls with toothpaste.** Toothpaste actually works well as a substitute for spackling paste. If you have just a few holes to fill or don't feel like making a run to the hardware store, fill tiny holes in drywall with a dab of plain white toothpaste. You can also color the toothpaste with food coloring to match paint colors.

# INDEX

# IMPROVE YOUR LIFE—
## One Hack at a Time!

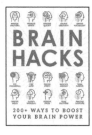